Singers of an Empty Day

"So let me sing of names remembered,
Because they, living not, can ne'er be dead,
Or long time take their memory quite away
From us poor singers of an empty day."

—William Morris: "The Earthly Paradise"

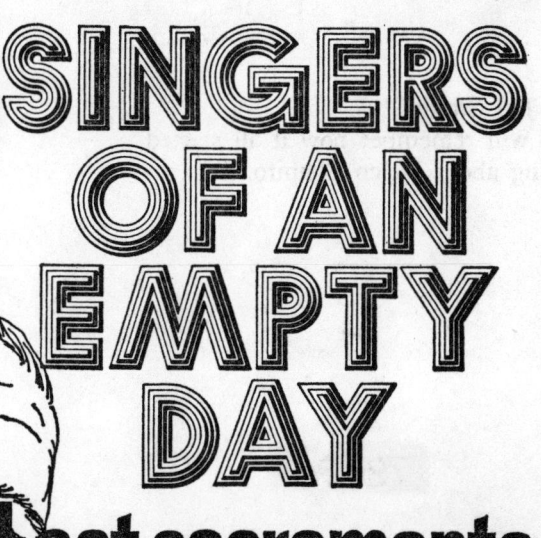

SINGERS OF AN EMPTY DAY

Last sacraments for the SUPERSTARS

****

KARL DALLAS

Illustrated by Gloria Dallas

KAHN & AVERILL

For Jeff Smith,
who will remember how it all started,
talking about Helen Shapiro.

First published in 1971 by Stanmore Press Ltd
under their associated imprint: Kahn & Averill.
Copyright © 1971 Karl Dallas.
This book may not be reproduced in whole or in
part without permission from the publishers.
Printed in England by
Willmer Brothers Limited, Birkenhead.

CONTENTS

The Assassination of Mick Jagger

"Honey - it's not one of those."
-*"Midnight Rambler"*

WE WERE lunching in Osteria San Lorenzo, the Yorkshire textiles man and I, when the young superstar brushed past our table, so close I could have touched him.

He looked at home in that environment. He looked to me like all the other too rich, too spoiled and slightly overworked young men one sees there. His hair had a careless contrivance that might have come out of the barber's on the other side of Beauchamp Place only a moment before. His immaculately cut double-breasted suit was obviously hand-tailored: one guessed Blades or Tommy Nutter. Like the rest of his kind, the open-neck shirt he wore with it was just a little too dressy to be casual. On his face was the slightly harassed, slightly amused look they all learn to wear even when they are terribly bored, *especially* when they are terribly bored.

The mouth was not quite as large, the lips not nearly as blubbery as in the libellous Scarfe cartoon, but it was still recognizably Mick Jagger.

'He looks even more revolting in the flesh than he does on the box,' said my companion with a shudder, before returning to his steak ('well done, please') and undressed salad, and to talk of tops and noils.

It was quite clear to me that we were seeing different people, and that to him the hate image created, initially, by the promotional genius of Peter Leslie and then brilliantly perpetuated by Jagger himself, was much more real than the soigné young man passing by our table. To me he was the same Jagger I knew from the Rolling Stones' top-floor office in Maddox Street, a man for whom the self-appointed role of drag queen evil genius of rock was just a job, something in which he had come to believe very deeply, as one does a myth, but nothing to do really with the day-to-day world of taxis and airline schedules and press receptions and lunch and dinner dates within which we coexisted most of the time.

Not only had my Yorkshire textiles man never considered Jagger at this level, but he was unable to believe it when he saw it before his very eyes. It was as if a tiny TV screen had interposed its own reality between the optic organ and the receiver in his head, reinterpreting what he saw in terms of what he knew to be true, however the immediate evidence of his senses might contradict it.

He was like a man wearing those trick spectacles which turn what he sees upside down. After a short while, the brain adjusts, and one day he finds the world has righted itself. He takes off the prismatic glasses to view the world as it really is and suddenly, – everything is upside down! (And by the way, remember that the way we actually see the world, it *is* upside down.)

My father-in-law says he would gladly take the Rolling Stones out and shoot them, and I know he means it. Given the chance, I know he would do it, and go back to play the piano in his Bradford pub quite contentedly.

Which is why Jagger was almost assassinated at the Altamont free concert, for the image is growing so much larger than the reality that even those who know and love him are beginning to believe that he is Satanic Majesty indeed, a devil asking ironically for your sympathy, a pop Baudelaire in love with the flowers of evil, practising magick. The hip media who know the real man behind the image so well have to turn away from this myth grown flesh, for it is truly terrifying, as if Charles Manson had gotten himself a rock and roll band.

Which is why they conspired together to hush up the attempts to kill him, though they put into proper perspective the events at Altamont, and instead went into the hysteria typified by Bill Graham's outraged statement to *Rolling Stone* magazine after the event: 'I'll ask you what right you had, Mr Jagger, to walk out on stage every night with your Uncle Sam hat, throw it down with complete disdain, and leave this country with $1.2 million? He's in his home country somewhere – what did he leave behind throughout the country? Every gig he was late. Every fucking gig he made the promoter and the people bleed. What right does this god have to descend on this country this way? It will give me great pleasure to tell the public that Mick Jagger is not God, Jr.'

Before the event, only a couple of weeks earlier, he had felt differently: 'What I hope the Stones do is turn the whole country on, wake 'em up. And I think the Stones can do it. Mick Jagger is the greatest fucking performer in the whole fucking world.' Of course, that was before the Altamont killing, when Graham was still counting up his 35 per cent of the $225,000 the Stones' first three concerts took at the gate.

When it comes to it, the hip community finds it just as hard to come to terms with Jagger's mythic reality as the straights, and the fact that they are intimate with another Jagger, the tired boy sprawling on the velvet sofa, the suddenly gentle smile, the long drawn-out Cockney *gro-o-o-o-a-a-a-a-n-n-n* of despair when someone asks for his opinion of the war in Vietnam, makes it all the harder.

Surely he's got to be putting us all on, isn't he, one minute coming on like Barbara Stanwyck and the next like the Boston strangler? I mean, it is all a con, isn't it, like Jim Morrison of the Doors unzipping his flies to wave his cock at the girls shrieking in the audience with wet knickers, like Jimi Hendrix wanking off his Fender Stratocaster, isn't it, a con, what he's doing up there, please?

Well yes, some of the time. But exactly where literal truth stops and mythic reality takes over can no longer be clear to anyone, least of all to Jagger himself, I imagine. The articulate boy debating Britain's narcotics laws with the Archbishop on an English country lawn after getting busted for blowing grass – that, surely is the real Jagger? Or is he still Mephistopheles, in one of his sneakier disguises, the devil quoting scriptures?

When he was making 'Performance' he began to dig wearing lipstick and paint so much he went around with it on his face off the set, and even when it was finally released, long years after he had moved on to other scenes, he reverted to the character of Turner from the movie for his TV interviews. Gone was the real Jagger (real?), the boy who knows exactly what he has to say and whose enunciation is so clear, London accent and all. The accent was broadened, all the h's and t's were abandoned, the words forced out of thick unwilling lips as if being formed for the first time by a slow, unwilling brain, the brows wrinkled with concentrated effort. Performance?

It is this blurring between illusion and reality which makes the life of a superstar so difficult, not the quest for non-existent privacy in a world where immediate contact, sought and unsought, is knocking down all physical barriers electronically for all of us. It is why Sinatra used to mash up photographers' cameras when they caught him with the wrong chick, why Janis Joplin was driven to die lonely in the Hollywood motel between sessions for her last record, why John Lennon takes the piss while making serious statements about starvation and war, why Bob Dylan spends more time creating an inscrutable dummy self to stand between him and his worshippers than he does making actual music. They booed him once when he exposed his electric soul to them, but never again, nossir.

For if we admit to ourselves, if only for a moment, that there is any truth in the myth, what else might not transpire? Just by mentioning the horrifying secret of the assassination attempts here, for instance, we make it more likely to be enacted in truth, for already there is some nut for whom this could be the crowning achievement of a nothing life, if only he could get himself together. Two Kennedys have gone, and Martin Luther King and Malcolm X. What better sacrifice could pop offer the world than to crucify its own devil incarnate?

When John Lennon said he was more popular than Jesus he was referring to the millions of Moslems, Hindus, Buddhists as well as Christians who liked his music, a statistical fact of life, let's admit it, but the Christians got uptight and burnt their Beatles records because they knew that in another way what he was saying was true. He wasn't claiming to be a Twentieth Century Jesus (and in fact, many of his otherwise inexplicable antics are a sort of insurance to save himself from crucifixion, for if a man lets his wife make films of his cock and exhibit them publicly, they are hardly likely to take him seriously enough to start driving in nails) but they suddenly realized that was exactly what he was becoming, and it threatened to cut the ground from under them. You can worship God and Mammon, as Rev Billy Graham and Richard Millhouse Nixon have shown us, but God and *God,* that's a bit too heavy.

When someone wrote to the *Melody Maker* saying 'Bob Dylan (and not, as previously reported, Jesus of Nazareth) is the living Messiah of today's young people' the Christians rose in rage. 'The main difference is: Bob Dylan will die. Jesus Christ will never die,' said John Corcoran of Bristol,

BS5 6JA, while J. B. Carroll of Stretford, Lancs complained that 'the Messiah is not someone who accumulates a fortune doing what he wants to do and then disappears at his whim to become a virtual recluse.'

As usual, Dylan had already had the last word: 'Being noticed can be a burden. Jesus got himself crucified because he got himself noticed. So I disappear a lot.'

Not enough, however, as the bootleg records prove. Despite the efforts of mechanical copyright protection societies and law enforcement agencies, they are on sale on the hip boulevards of the western world, badly pressed, unlabelled albums in plain white covers, sometimes with a title hand-stencilled, never the name of the artist: 'Stealin' ', 'Great White Wonder', 'LiveR Than You'll Ever Be', 'Get Back'. Some of them betray their origins from internal evidence: the bootleg Hendrix was obviously taken off 'Top of the Pops' by the tinny TV-type sound. Others are more mysterious. 'LiveR' seems to be from the Stones' concert at the Oakland Coliseum during their 1969 American tour, and the quality of the stereo is so high that it has got to have been taken straight out of the Stones' own mixer, on stage. There were persuasive suggestions of collusion by the Stones, which were not dispelled when Jagger described the quality of the 'official' live record, 'Get Yer Ya-Yas Out', as 'even better than the bootleg'.

Actually, there is more sense of immediacy on the bootleg record, probably because it has not been subjected to the same process of re-mixing and balancing. This tinkering can result in perfect product, but less-than-perfect art. A good example of such interference is 'Get Back', a bootleg album which is presumably what 'Let It Be' sounded like before Phil Spector exploded it into a typically over-blown, over-produced product of his own technological megalomania. The original is not good Beatles, and the divisions which ended them up in the law courts are already beginning to show, but it is real Beatles, while the Spector re-mix is purest plastic, from run-in groove to centre hole.

What is really at issue here is the right of the artist to control his own output, to decide what he considers fit for his public's consumption. Some bootlegs are simple violations of the copyright laws (which Castro repealed as one of the first acts of the Cuban Revolution, incidentally; think about it), and some are even illegal dubbings of discs which are already commercially available. But they are untypical. People really buy bootlegs to hear things that don't have the approval of the artist. The man who buys a bootleg is asserting the right of consumer control of the arts.

Typical is the first bootleg of all, which naturally had to be by Dylan, of all pop musicians the most assiduous in preserving his legal and contractual rights as artist, the most unwilling to allow past achievements to confuse his present artistic direction (or to clarify the confusion he himself spreads as some sort of self-protective mechanism). Like any Stalinist historian, he tries all the time to rewrite his musical biography so that it conforms with where he's at now, appearing to follow a simple linear direction, from protest folk to electric rock to country-styled easy listenin'. Each time he moves on to a new stage, it seems anything previously recorded but so far unissued has to stay that way, so no one gets confused.

The fact that his newest listeners have only just joined the ride, that they were six or seven years old when the trip started, that one of these kids is just as likely to start with a recent Dylan and work his way back historically to that raw, rough, terrible first vital album, possibly skipping the phase between 'Bringing It All Back Home' and 'Blonde on Blonde' to pick up on them later, makes nonsense of this effort. These kids have grown up in a world where Dylan is an accepted, tangible fact of musical historiography, but still he tries to keep the unmanageable process under control.

He hasn't got round yet, like Roualt, to burning material he doesn't approve of (Columbia probably wouldn't let him) but I do believe he's working on it. He'll have to work fast, however, for there are already too many things he can't destroy. The bootlegs are part of a participatory process by which the audience is choosing what they want from his creations, perhaps preferring to listen to the unissued 'Tears of Rage' rather than to his rendition of 'Blue Moon' on 'Self Portrait', whatever point he was trying to make by dragging out the tired old old-style pop standard.

It's an interesting fact that the bootleg Dylans didn't come out during the period of his long silence, although that may be because the guts of all of them was recorded then.

The silence was only partly voluntary. Dr Freud says there are no accidents and who are we to contradict him, so perhaps that day when he flew off his motorbike and broke his neck, who knows, perhaps it wasn't such an accident after all. He told John Cohen that he came to the conclusion there had to be something else to do besides touring, just going out there performing the songs while everyone else was having a good time, being pushed on stage and carried out. Anyway, the smash broke his neck and produced 'Wheel's On Fire', one of his most terrifying songs, he got married, and disappeared. No more tours. No more concerts. No more records.

Another factor was his fear and dislike of the influence he was exerting on pop musicians. He once confided in Louis Killen, the Geordie ballad-singer, that when he swung from folk to rock he was dismayed to find that all the young folkies did likewise, swapping their Martin acoustics for Fenders. He had discovered a basic fact about mass communications media: that they create electronic mirrors in front of which a whole generation can reflect itself. A global tribe, all marching to the beat of the different drummer. For a while, and it seemed that it was going to be for ever, Dylan had dropped the drumsticks

But, as Brecht says, teaching without pupils is difficult. The writer has to get his stuff out, listened to and sung, and so he and his friends started to jam together, in the basement of his home in Woodstock, NY, trying out some of the new songs he was beginning to write out of his new-healed head. The friends were a rock-and-roll band that had recorded with an Arkansas singer called Ronnie Hawkins: an incredible young Canadian guitarist called Robbie Robertson, who had done remarkable things at the age of 19 on Hawkins' 1963 revival of the old Bo Diddley hit, 'Who Do You Love?', Levon Helm on drums, Garth Hudson on organ, Richard Manuel on piano, and Rick Danko on bass. They had played with Dylan on his last tour and they were staying with him in Big Pink, his Woodstock home, and they began to put together some songs to send round to people who might like to record them. The basement tape.

Manfred Mann did 'Mighty Quinn'. Julie Driscoll had a hit with 'Wheel's On Fire'. Sandy Denny did Dylan's song to Nico, 'I'll Keep It With Mine', with Fairport Convention before she left them. Eventually the friends, now known simply as The Band, did 'Wheel's On Fire' as well, the definitive version.

Well ... not quite. The definitive version is the one we were not meant to hear, by the author. Copies were made of copies of copies of the basement tape. It was a sign of in-ness to have one of those lo-fi tapes. Somewhere there, the man could be heard under the hiss and static and hum, singing. This was at the time when he had completely disappeared from public view, become a myth, canonized. We might never see nor hear from him again. Even his manager had to communicate with him by way of a third party, an old friend from his earliest folk days. The rumours flourished: the accident had left him a cripple, a deaf mute, a vegetable idiot lobotomized by the asphalt scalpel of the roadway. But there he was, singing. The hopeful slogan was being chalked on subway walls: DYLAN LIVES.

The basement tape was the basis for most of the Dylan bootlegs. But there is a lot more other Dylan around than he is prepared to have out on official Columbia records, not to mention the songs that were censored off his first album, like the highly political 'Talking John Birch Society Blues'. There were demo tapes he'd done for Witmark Publishing, heart of the Tin Pan Alley establishment, a whole Carnegie Hall concert recorded by Columbia and never released, and most particularly recordings he made during his European tour with the Band (still then, remembering their apprenticeship with Ronnie Hawkins, calling themselves the Hawks). That was the tour when the audiences booed him for selling out and playing electric, not understanding that he'd started out as a rocker, that the folk phase was something he went through, his brief obeisance to the East Coast liberal-Marxist establishment still so powerful in show biz, before getting it on musically.

One of those performances with the Hawks, recorded before an audience in Liverpool, for God's sake, in 1966, was sneaked out as the B-side of 'I Want You' and is still available, but only in Europe. Dylan has frequently pointed out that his records don't give much of an impression of what he's really like on stage, and he's right. But that doesn't explain why he doesn't allow the rest of the Liverpool concert to be heard, or that first Carnegie Hall show.

Mike Wadleigh told me he kept Janis Joplin's performances out of the film 'Woodstock' because they were so shitty, and probably she preferred it that way, but anyone who knew Janis knew she could vary between incredible and incredibly bad, according to mood. The shitty performances were just as much a part of her as any takes that might catch Wadleigh's approval, or mine or yours.

Actually, this idea of the artist as a man apart, the man up there in the spotlight, and us down here contributing our little 'Sieg Heil' choruses to the genius who knows exactly what's best for us, is quite a modern idea. And if the sage McLuhan is right, and the replacement of print by electronics is bringing us all back home to the tribal collective, it's already out of date. Artists didn't begin to sign their works until the Renaissance, until the printing press had made them realize they could be businessmen, but Britain's Performing Right Society didn't institutionalize the process until 1914. *'My name is nothing extry, so that I will not tell,'* sang the old folk singers, speaking as many-to-many not one-to-all. Composer John Cage pointed out that the idea of an artist 'expressing himself' would have been regarded as heretical before the Renaissance, and it's ironic that it should have been at Woodstock, where Dylan lived for a time (currently he has a house in Macdougall Street, Greenwich Village) that Cage first performed his silent work, '4 minutes 33 seconds' in 1952, about nine years before Dylan cut his first records as an anonymous mouth-organist with Big Joe Williams and Victoria Spivey. Ironic, because Cage had already discovered you just can't do anything you want.

Seeking silence, Cage got himself put in the sound-insulated anechoic room at Harvard – and was well-nigh deafened by the high-pitched whistle of his nervous system and the low thunder of his blood, pulsing. That day in Woodstock, the pianist closed his instrument at the beginning of each movement, and the audience listened instead to the sounds from the woods behind the hall, the patter of raindrops on the roof, and to their own voices, as they began to mutter among themselves in perplexity. Audience participation equals consumer power!

Rock musicians have begun to flash upon what Cage is at – 'Revolution No 9' on the Beatles' white album is one of the less successful attempts at aleatory pop music – but not many of them have really dug that what he is saying is that their music doesn't belong to them at all. Hence the bootlegs.

Of course, like everything else in pop culture, bootlegs are wrapped up in commerce. More, since they are

B

pricier than regular records and no one but the presser and the distributors gets paid, they are more of a rip-off than normal products of the straight business state's pop-industrial complex. But the illegality, if nothing else, stops them from evolving the sort of alien corporate structures which eat at the heart of any alternative culture. Even if they stay out of court, no bootleg kings are going to make the Beatles' mistake of setting up an Apple Corps, though it is significant that one of the first projects Apple set their electronic wizzkid was a device to make it impossible to dub copy tapes from discs or radio broadcasts. It doesn't seem to have worked.

It's tough shit being a demi-god. The history of god-heads and kingship and priesthood and bardic crowns is littered with the bones of divine victims who didn't want to climb up on to their crosses, Joans who didn't want to be burnt, Dylan Thomases and Brendan Behans who tried so hard not to drink themselves to death.

The Norse sagas tell the story of one Tenth Century divine monarch, King Hakon, who got converted to Christianity and refused to take part in pagan rituals, and wouldn't eat the sacred horseflesh at Yuletime. He was told to eat up his horse's liver or make way for another king. He ate.

During the Sicilian drought of 1893, Sir James Frazer tells us, the peasants prayed for rain. When the skies stayed cloudless for six months they took the saints out of the churches and chucked them on to the dungheaps, tore their wings off, and dressed them in sack-cloth. St Angelo of Licata was even threatened with hanging if he didn't make it rain.

Man created God in his own image, and He better remember it, or there'll be, literally, hell to pay. The idea of a god who could do exactly what he wanted, without any reference to the needs and wishes of humanity, is quite a modern invention. Primitive man, who knew that each year he had to slay the corngod made flesh, and plant him in the ground so that he could rise up again, not in three days but with the harvest next autumn, knew equally well that neither he nor the corngod had any choice or free will in the matter. The corn had to grow and be cut down, and the corngod had to be sacrificed, so it could all come to pass.

They are all sacrifices, whether they bleed to death at the gates of an all-white hospital like Bessie Smith, or they plunge to their death in a plummeting plane like Buddy Holly and Big Bopper and Otis Redding and Ritchie Valens, or their car careers off the road like Eddie Cochran, Bertha Chippie Hill, Jay B. Perkins, Martin Lamble, Clifford Brown, and Frank Teschmaker, or perish in the bath, balling, like Jim Morrison, his over-strained heart pumping to explode under the strain of the death-fated speeded-up and barbiturated-down life of a pop superstar, the self-consciously mythic lizard king himself, finding his end not like Oedipus killing his father and fucking his mother, but in a Paris hotel bathroom, suddenly flopping into the puke and cum-filled dirty bathwater, dead; another sacrifice.

The torment of the modern superstar is this: he is a god in a new time of myth, whether he likes it or not, whether he knows it or not. He's got the choice, to come down from Olympus or be crucified. That's why superstars are becoming harder to find these days. It isn't every rock-and-roll singer who wants to get himself assassinated.

II

Mr. Nixon's Capo

"And now, the end is near ..."
    –My Way

JUST AFTER the war, fresh out of school, fired with United Nations Charter idealism and convinced of my own invulnerability, I joined Sir Oswald Mosley's newly-revived fascists as a self-appointed undercover agent. A crazy thing to do, especially for someone with relatives who remembered the bloody stage productions that had been Mosley's pre-war meetings, with the police as non-disinterested spectators. I did manage to louse up a few of their carefully-planned emergences from under the stones before I blew my cover, but all that happened was they came round and threatened to smash my mother's windows in. She got rid of them, easily.

Before that happened, when they were beginning my political education, the first thing they said I must do was to throw away my cherished Frank Sinatra records. The man was a Communist, they said, not so obvious but therefore even more dangerous than Paul Robeson. The young man who told me all this, I recall, confided also that he slept on a black satin pillow embroidered with a swastika, and informed me that the gas ovens at Buchenwald had been for refuse disposal.

I had never seen Sinatra in this light, though to be sure his haunting 'All or Nothing At All' had stirred echoes in my teenage heart, symbolizing a decisive change in mood from the 'Buddy Can You Spare a Dime' resignation of pre-war depression. It had not been the words so much, though their nihilistic totalism had a definite appeal, but rather the way the intense, adolescent voice was counter-pointed by the brass-dominated Harry James band, surrounding the lyrics with haunting visions of hot, self-destructive passion. To be sure, this was more realistic love than the pap our parents doted on, so it's easy to see that in the new generation game of them and us, Sinatra was definitely us. An erotic politician, years before Jim Morrison.

Today, when Sinatra is rooting for Ronald Rayguns in California and echoing the President's disgust at the long-haired bums without the sense to avoid getting themselves dead on American campuses in defence of faraway places with Oriental-sounding names, it's hard to recall how we young rebels identified with him, the guy who took on the establishment on his own terms and won, most of the time. Is this chubby, talcummed real-estate tycoon with the new hairpiece the man who used to have Jack Kennedy's photo on his desk, inscribed 'to my friend', who told us about the rocks slung at him and the other Italian kids during his Hoboken childhood, and made us feel with him the psychological scars as deep as the forceps marks left on his neck during his clumsy birth?

Is this the same gangling, goggle-eyed youth whose singing of 'The House I Live In' was of a piece with 'Ballad of Americans' and all those other sweet hymns of peace and love which were the Forties versions of the equally illusory Sixties flower power daydreams? The parents of today's long-haired bums could have been among the 30,000 Sinatra-struck bobbysoxers who rampaged through New York on Columbus Day in 1944 – a year in which, incidentally, his earnings reached nearly one and a half million dollars, a 2,000 per cent increase on the 125 dollars a week he got when he joined Tommy Dorsey four years previously. This was the world's first experience of teenage power, long before the 'Rock Around the Clock' riots had them tearing the seats out of the cinemas and dancing in the aisles in Times Square and Tottenham Court Road.

There seemed to be something qualitatively different between Sinatra and all the singers who'd gone before. Never mind Jack Leonard, the nowhere singer whose chair with the Tommy Dorsey band he'd taken over; Sinatra had something quite distinct from the top man himself, homely, pipe-smoking, golf-playing Bing Crosby. The business hadn't changed that much, though, and on the face of it they seemed to have more in common than the warring factions of fans cared to admit. Like Crosby, Sinatra had come out of the big band swing scene, though Paul Whiteman making a lady out of that honky-tonk harlot, jazz, had been beginning something and Harry James and Tommy Dorsey (and Benny Goodman, with whom Sinatra shared the bill on his first solo concert) were bringing it to an end, even if we didn't know it yet. Sinatra also sang with a vocal group as Crosby had done in his big band days, backing up Dorsey's chick singer, Jo Stafford, as one of the Pied Pipers.

He had even worked as a (badly paid) song-plugger in the days before Harry James discovered him singing for pennies in the Rustic Cabin, a club in New Jersey. The music industry still had very little realization of the new electronics growing up around them, which they saw basically as just a means of getting more people into the music stores to buy the words and piano accompaniments of their favourite songs. Records were not yet so important. That's how long it takes your average show-biz tycoon to realize which way is up: Nashville's WSM had been churning out hillbilly pop since the mid-1920s, changing the whole sound of country music not once but several times, but of course that was hardly worth bothering about. The family of Mr A. P. Carter had only sold a mere ten million records for Victor, most of them outside the big cities, thanks to the power of the phonograph and the radio. Few of those hicks from the sticks could even read and write simple American, never mind crochets and quavers, so the significance of what was going on below the Mason-Dixon line somehow escaped the wise old men of Tin Pan Alley.

As a result, Sinatra's big radio show, 'The All-Time Hit Parade' listed not the best-selling records, as you might expect today, but the sheet music. (And if you think we're so much smarter now, please bear in mind that the basic format of our 'Top of the Pops' TV show is based on sales of singles, with a tiny token ackowledgement that the whole economy of pop music is now geared to the sales of long-play albums.) However, though they didn't understand it, American show business did at least do something to exploit some of the potential of electronics, if only as a sales aid. Because of the radio monopoly in Britain, based on a power structure nearly a century old, British commercial music was a much clearer example of a culture based upon print, which it continued to be, right up to the time when the Beatles smashed their little world into fragments of shellac.

What this means can be gathered, perhaps, from a short digression on the origins of Britain's Tin Pan Alley. The real name of the street is Denmark Street. It runs from Charing Cross Road to St Giles's Church, which now stands on the site of an old leper hospital. Condemned men used to pause there for prayer or a drink at the nearby tavern on their way from Newgate to Tyburn to be hanged. Just down the road is Seven Dials, nicknamed Grub Street, where cheap printers like Johnny Pitts and Jemmy Catnach used to rush out ballads on the latest execution, or the horrible unsolved murder almost (but not quite) too bloody to relate. They were sold on the streets like newspapers by 'screamers' and 'running patterers'. These ruffians, who often told of gory details quite missing from their wares, and sold their longer songs by the yard, were the first song-pluggers.

The first respectable publisher to set up in Denmark Street itself, Lawrence Wright, built his fortunes on one of those old ballads, a maudlin ditty called 'Don't go Down the Mine Daddy', which he bought for five pounds from a singer in the street outside. A few weeks later a mine explosion killed 136 men and Wright rushed out an edition of the song, selling a million copies in three weeks.

Tin Pan Alley was thus founded on this single narrative ballad, a tear-jerker if there ever was one – which is perhaps why the type of moon-and-June lovesong now sung by only a few survivals of a dead age like Andy Williams and Tom Jones and Engelbert Humperdinck is still called a 'ballad' in the trade, though technically they are lyric songs.

David Day of Francis, Day and Hunter in nearby Charing Cross Road thought up the gimmick of selling songs to music hall performers for two guineas a song, giving each one the exclusive right to sing his song on stage, plus a third of the royalties. Later Mr Day helped form the Performing Right Society to administer the royalty system that grew up around this little scheme.

Though there are differences, this British model was basically the same as the industry into which Sinatra erupted that New Year's Eve in 1942 when he shared the bill with Benny Goodman and a Bing Crosby movie. He sang the same old songs, mostly, but in a way that made the girls wriggle in near-orgasm. It wasn't so much what he sang, but the way he sang it, wringing out of the banalities suggestions of something too exciting to be put into literal words. Commentators trying to understand what the hell was going on suggested it was his 'little boy lost' appeal that turned the ladies on, but they themselves knew better. The mouth inside the unbuttoned blouses of their daydreams was no baby's. Long before Actors' Studio, Sinatra was applying the Stanislavsky method to some of the corniest material since Little Nell, turning the songs into something almost believable, into dreams that were far from chaste.

At the same time, something had happened to Sinatra. It was one thing to use electronics to get on more intimate terms with his audience, involving them in his fantasy, playing on the ribs of their emotions like a xylophone. It was when they responded in like terms, getting into his private life in a way that had been denied the fans of a previous sex-symbol from a different technology, filmdom's Rudolph Valentino. It was one thing to dedicate 'Nancy With the Laughing Face' to the daughter of that other Nancy, the girl he'd married in Jersey City in February 1939. When he divorced her twelve years later, they wouldn't let him stop singing the damn song!

The girls who tore bits off his clothes could be handled by bodyguards, but as they grew up and out into blue-rinsed moms making goo-goo eyes at him as they queued at his table whenever he dropped into a club for a quiet drink and a meal, as they slipped fattening arms over his shoulders to breathe innocent salaciousnesses into his violated ears, they were harder to handle. The men were no easier, for his reputation as a randy-dandy stud made him a phantom cuckolder to every man whose wife was turning away from him to project on to the bedroom wall her dreams of what might have been. Sinatra met hostility with hostility.

About then, he began going down. It was not merely that the little boy was getting bigger, the boney face rather fatter round the chops. The emotional intensity he poured into his songs was as strong as ever, but in comparison with the histrionics of the guys who took the emotional bit and cranked it up even higher, it sounded weaker, compared with Frankie Laine, for instance, and in particular Johnnie Ray, the poor deaf boy who used to break down into floods of real tears on stage, selling over a million copies of 'The Little White Cloud That Cried' in eight weeks. That was the year Sinatra married Ava Gardner, just eight days after divorcing Nancy, 1951. A year later he was an out-of-work nobody hanging round his wife's locations. Husband of the star – what a comedown!

Once again, the music business was changing radically, and still hardly anyone realized what was going on. The long-play album and the higher fidelity possible with singles revolving at 45 rpm was creating needs neither the industry nor the big-band singers like Sinatra, Perry Como, Dean Martin, Al Martino, could satisfy. Instead, the white kids were getting their kicks from black rhythm and blues, wherever and whenever they were fortunate enough to have a local radio station playing the stuff (which was never, if you lived in Britain).

When Alan Freed, a classical music disc jockey in Cleveland, Ohio, heard the kids playing the records of unknowns like Red Prysock and Ivory Joe Hunter at the opening of Leo Mintz's new record store in 1952, he realized that something was happening and he didn't know what it was, did he, Mr Jones?

Freed started a rhythm and blues show aimed at the white audience, and when he hired the Cleveland Arena for a live version of 'Moondog's Rock and Roll Party', most of the audience were white. Tin Pan Alley – the area around New York's 47th Street – seemed as if it was going to be superseded by Tenth Avenue between 42nd and 56th, home of the independent record companies who were alive to a new kind of music that the major record companies, carrying around their vast corporate structures like old men of the sea, were unable to handle. When Bill

Haley's 'Crazy Man Crazy' began zooming up the Billboard charts in 1953, the disc jockeys obliged the majors by playing their effete cover version by Ralph Marterie, but it was still the Haley version for Essex, an independent company, that made it.

The majors weren't about to allow that situation to continue, and so by the end of the year Decca had bought Bill Haley, and he was recording 'Rock Around the Clock', which was in the top ten for 19 weeks, including eight at the number one spot. Haley was a pretty watered-down version of the black music he was appropriating, but it was a beginning nevertheless of something that didn't really have much room in it for Sinatra's style. Pat Boone could compromise by doing cover versions of rock 'n' roll hits, fairly successfully in fact, though he went back to old-style 'ballads' as soon as r&r had established his name with the kids. But Sinatra's image was pretty set – and it was fading.

Nineteen fifty-three, the year of rock 'n' roll in America. The year of skiffle in Britain. A new kind of music for white youth which hadn't yet produced its demi-gods – Elvis cut his first record for Sun of Memphis a year later – but which represented something remarkable and frightening in the industry. Before, they had decided what records the public would have an opportunity to buy, and gave them a selection to choose from. That's the way politics is still run, of course, with the voter who doesn't want to vote for either of the bi-partisan policies offered him voluntarily disenfranchising himself, with the added indignity of being labelled apathetic to boot. Like most heavy industries, politics has been rather slow to waken up to what's been happening.

The consumer revolution! If the majors didn't want to give them the choice they wanted, they could sneak into the ghetto for some black rhythm and blues discs, or twist the dial looking for the black radio stations. In Britain, the absence of black radio stations made it even easier, pushing the kids towards their own music-making. You made a tea-chest into a makeshift double bass, borrowed mum's washboard, bought yourself a cheap Spanish guitar, and you had the makings of a skiffle group. The musical establishment, from the entertainment combines to the musicians' trade union, reacted against the new music with rage and disgust, for many were the vested interests on both sides.

Perhaps realizing that his was one of them, Sinatra did a remarkably far-sighted thing. Instead of competing, as Pat Boone was doing, he astounded everyone by leaving music, to take the part of the cheerful loser, Maggio, in 'From Here to Eternity' for eight thousand dollars. Whoever it was at MGM who decided to give him the part must have had the genius to penetrate to the heart of exactly where Sinatra was at, or perhaps it was merely that in the film test Sinatra had done what he always tended to do, like any Method actor, projecting the misery he had been experiencing at the time into the part. Always remember that to take the film test Sinatra had to fly back from Africa, where he'd been kicking his heels around the 'Mogambo' set. In retrospect, it seems so obvious that you'd think the part had been tailormade for Sinatra: the game and loveable underdog who gets beaten up by the heavy. It was a part Sinatra had played all his life, but this time it won him an Oscar.

Not that Sinatra was new to cinema. He was in films almost before he was much of a record name, singing 'All or Nothing At All' in a short about the music business called 'Reveille with Beverly'. The movie's success in Europe was limited, perhaps, by the fact that we called it 'Revally with Beverly', which doesn't have quite the same ring-a-ding-ding to it. One of his later movies, 'On the Town,' with music by Leonard Bernstein, couldn't be excluded from any filmography with pretensions to document the history of the musical. But rarely had they portrayed the Sinatra under the skin, the one the girls had swooned over, which is what they did with Maggio.

It was, in a way, the end of an era, for Maggio was a memory of the past. Out of the depths of his despair, down as far as he could get, Sinatra was about to dredge a new, less vulnerable character. No longer the down-trodden put-upon, this brittle-bright, wisecracking, alienated bastard went by various names but was best exemplified by the character of Pal Joey. As originally envisaged by John O'Hara's story, Joey was a despicable gigolo who lived off women. In the movie this rather questionable aspect of his character was glossed over and a ridiculous out-of-character happy ending was tacked on.

No one was fooled, nor even very much worried, for the new Sinatra had plenty of sex appeal. There were plenty of women who'd have been glad to keep a tame Sinatra stashed away in the bedroom closet for use when needed. He wasn't the old Sinatra, he was nothing like a little boy lost, but nor was he yet the tired old reactionary he has now become. He still had sympathies for causes, but it was no longer because he needed it himself, even psychologically: he offered it to the under-privileged, among whom he had no great wish to be numbered.

So he campaigned for jolly Jack Kennedy, the embodiment of all the liberal virtues, promising so much but producing so little, the millionaire's son who seemed to be offering an alternative to the used car hucksterism of Nixon, and instead let the CIA involve his country in the Bay of Pigs fiasco, and whose greatest achievement was in taking the world to the brink of war over the Cuban missiles – and then to bring it back again.

Like the celebrated Mr K, jumping through a hogshead of real fire!

The aging white middle-class was making its last bid in favour of gradualness as a tactic to avoid anything that might threaten their position in the structure. At that time, the most important thing was to contain the black nationalist movement and keep it on safe, liberal lines, constituting no fundamental threat to the system. In the guise of the Civil

Rights movement they succeeded, for a time. Later, of course, the revolutionary movement had spread to their own children, and the music of their rebellion was rock and roll.

That really came later, for rock 'n' roll the commercial, exploitive product had not yet become rock and roll the revolutionary art form of white urban youth. Sinatra changed record companies, and began to make discs that expressed perfectly the middle-class dream of the Fifties, a romantic cynicism firmly based upon an unreal but existing dream world of night clubs, booze, and rather messy love affairs. While his earlier records for Columbia had been lushly orchestrated by Axel Stordahl, at Capitol he found a new orchestra-leader, an ex-trombonist from the Dorsey band called Nelson Riddle. After his teeth went and he left the Dorsey brass section, Riddle had done some pretty romantic arrangements himself, notably 'Mona Lisa', which swung Nat 'King' Cole from being a jazzy singer-pianist in the Earl Hines style, with his own lightly jumping combo, into a soft and husky Negro crooner. But, for Sinatra, Riddle put in more of a bounce, with frequent trumpet obbligati from Harry Edison, a jazzman whose nickname, 'Sweets', showed he wasn't from the more strident school of hornmen, however.

There was still angst aplenty, for what Sinatra was selling was a sort of masochistic self-criticism which was exemplified by Johnny Mercer's 'One for My Baby (and One More for the Road)'. As performed by Sinatra in clubs and on concert dates, it was a brilliant coup de theatre to finish the first half on a downbeat note just before the intermission. Usually with all the house lights out, smoking a cigarette whose smoke spidered upwards through the solitary spot, Sinatra, leaning on Bill Miller's piano, played the archetypal maudlin drunk who's last out of the bar, afraid to face the night and go home because there's no one to go home to and face it with. In the last chorus he'd turn away from mike and walk off, so his final words were lost to the microphone, a musical gesture of resigned futility accompanied by the applause of an audience moved to tears by the sadness, the sheer inevitability of it all, an individual instance of the terrible state the world was in, and no one could do anything about it.

It's reported that when Sinatra recorded the song for his 'No One Cares' album, A&R man Dave Cavenaugh had all the lights turned out in the studio and lit Sinatra by a single spot, just like in the clubs. And it was done in one take, as if it were a live show.

The part that booze played in the middle-class culture for whom Sinatra became a spokesman is just one of the strong cultural differences between the generations, for today's pot-smoking youth regard Sinatra's inevitable Jack Daniels and a little water with as much distaste as most parents look upon dope. The fact that one of their own demi-gods, Janis Joplin, also used booze as a stage prop is regarded as a loveable eccentricity.

That self-appointed puritanical guardian of the revolutionary conscience, Frank Zappa, has never so accurately documented this anti-hedonism as in his 'America Drinks and Goes Home', in which a night club singer of obvious derivation tries to get the customers to go home with the sort of soliloquy that can still be heard today in the older people's drinking joints: 'This is a special request. I hope you enjoy it.

> '*I tried to find how my heart could be so blind dear*
> *How could I be fooled just like the rest?*
> *You came on strong with your fast car and your class*
> *   ring*
> *Soft voice and your sad eyes, I fell for the whole thing.*
> *I don't regret having met up with a girl*
> *Who breaks hearts like they were nothing at all.*
> *I've done it too, now I know just what it feels like,*
> *And (just like I said) there's no regrets.*

'It's now time to close. I hope you've had as much fun as we have. Don't forget the jam session Sunday. Mandy Tension will be by, playing his xylophone troupe. It'll be a lot of fun.

'Monday night is the dance contest night. Twist contest. We give away peanut butter and jelly.

'I hope we've played your requests, the songs you like to hear.

'Last call for alcohol. Drink it up folks. Wonderful.

'Nice to see you Bob. How's it going? Wonderful. Nice to see you. "Oh Bill Bailey"? We'll get to that tomorrow. "Caravan" with the drum solo? Right. We'll do that. Wonderful. Nice to see you again. Yeh, la la la. Down at the Pompadour A-go-go.

' 'Night all.'

The record closes with screams and the noise of smashing tables and crockery as the patrons bust the joint up, before going home.

Zappa himself describes this cut as 'an unsubtle parody of adult conduct in neighbourhood cocktail lounges in America'. He says: 'The humour is aimed at (1) the type of music your parents like to listen to, (2) the manner in which they like to have it performed (the insincerity of the night-club crooner in his closing address to the alcoholics at the bar), (3) the manner in which the audience persists in talking above the level of the music while it is being performed . . .'

Meanwhile, time isn't standing still. The contradictions are getting tougher. The mild requests of the Civil Rightsers, the constitutional procedures of the Supreme Court which had outlawed segregation in schools back in 1954, were being met by white riots and bombings. The polite white rock 'n' roll of Bill Haley, so tough-sounding in the context of the early Fifties, was sounding weak and watery in comparison with black musicians who could tell the music like it really was. In songs like Ray Charles's frenetic, gospel-inspired 'What'd I say?' in 1959, the new mood was

c

aggressively obvious, but these singers were also invading Sinatra's own natural territory, the sentimental ballad.

In a Sinatra song, the sex had always been implied. And it was the sort of a romance that began with roses every day by special messenger, lunch in the Hotel Plaza, went on with him buying chic clothes for the chick on Fifth Avenue, dinner at the Four Seasons, dancing at Max's Kansas City, and finishing up (one assumed) with bed in his Playboy pad. You used your imagination. Norman Mailer's American wet dream. Instead, the new songs took the realities of the thing for granted, talked of women bringing their men breakfast in bed, suggested unmentionable pleasures (*'over the hill and way down underneath'*), joked bitterly about their chicks making it with the iceman while they were at work, and even commented directly upon their own sexual inabilities.

The musical establishment had been getting uptight for a long time about this side of rock. After all, even the very words 'jazz' and 'rock'n'roll' were originally argot ways of saying 'fuck'. Bill Haley had said: 'We steer clear of anything suggestive.' So he dropped the 'over the hill' verse from his version of 'Shake Rattle and Roll', but it wasn't any use, the audience knew what the song was about anyway. It was rather like the Rev Sabine Baring-Gould, the Somerset folk song collector who was so shocked by the rape in 'Blow Away the Morning Dew' that he wrote completely new verses, leaving the chorus intact. The singers who gave it to him must have smiled, if they heard their kids singing the bowdlerized version at school, for they knew that 'morning dew (as also in 'The Foggy Dew') meant sperms.

As pop entered the Sixties, the great American romance had to face up to a few facts, and once more Sinatra hit a trough. This time his audience wasn't reacting in quite the same monolithic way, for the new media were creating new inter-relationships between different types of people that were much more complex than the press, either underground or overground, tried to make out. It was obvious, furthermore, that a time was coming for even the middle class to stand up and be counted.

There didn't seem to be an artistic solution. Instead, Sinatra bought himself a piece of the remaining action, quitting Columbia and setting up his own corporation, Reprise. Since his voice was obviously deteriorating, it was an intelligent thing to do, except that no man can get as involved in business as Sinatra did and emerge artistically unscathed. Even the Beatles have discovered that now.

As Robin Douglas-Home, one of his most devoted and almost sycophantic fans, recorded shortly after, 'Apart from owning Reprise records, with its four million dollar sales in the first year of its existence, he owns Essex Productions. . . . He runs four music publishing companies. He is co-partner with Danny Kaye in a string of radio stations in the Pacific North-West. He has bought and re-styled a hotel-casino near Reno, Nevada. He is vice-president and a major stockholder in the Sands Hotel, Las Vegas. . . . His various projects are said to gross somewhere around twenty million dollars a year.' Not surprisingly, Douglas-Home had to admit that 'he might not be putting as much time and effort into his albums as he should'.

From there on it was all downhill. Having started out poor, made a lot as part of the avant garde of the youth revolution, lost some of it during the temporary truce at the end of the Forties, and made it back again, he played safe on making it from then on. He was secure, and any-one who rocked the boat was a bum. It was one thing to expend incredible efforts to raise money for humanitarian causes, like the over one million dollars he raised for children's charities during his world tour of the early Sixties. But it was quite something else to countenance anything which might, just possibly, bring tumbling down the whole edifice of night clubs and plush hotels and penthouse suites, and doorbells marked 'You'd better have a damn good reason for ringing this bell'.

Unfair, perhaps, to sling mud at him, for he was a child of his time. Look at them all, the liberal-Marxists, the jazzmen, the poets in the International Brigade, the personalities, the statesmen with umbrellas, from that era, they knew all the answers but they weren't asking the right questions. Some of them died for us, a lot of them took a lot of our parents' generation to the grave with them, but all in all they fucked it up.

Artistically, Sinatra's real tragedy was that he survived. If, like so many other singers from the big band era, he had declined into infrequently interrupted obscurity, he would never have had to cope with the changes that the new media were imposing upon popular culture.

When he started out, the business was based on print, essentially sheet music oriented. But the power of electronics which took his voice into the homes of the world also created a need for feedback, the hunger for personal minutiae which put the newshounds on his trail, and got a lot of reporters' noses punched, a lot of photographers' cameras smashed.

You'd better have a damn good reason for ringing this bell. That gives the clue. Sinatra wanted to stay his own man. He ended up being his corporations' baby.

III

Meanwhile, in Vegas . . .

"Waal, it's one for the money,
Two for the show,
Three to get ready,
Now go cat go . . ."
                    –Blue Suede Shoes

HE LOOKS a little like Rod Steiger as the sheriff in 'In the Heat of the Night': a beer belly, and chomping a cigar, supervising the pinning up of candyfloss decorations all over Las Vegas, ten days before the arrival of the king. *This* is the man who created a legend? It is indeed, Col. Tom Parker as ever was, the man under whose control Elvis Presley was developed, like any piece of real estate, out of the aggressive paranoia of 'Blue Suede Shoes', through the throat-throbbing vibrato of 'Love Me Tender', via too many B-script movies, terrible wastes of talent most of them, by way of nine years of legendary isolation, to a position where he can sell out the 2,000 seats of the Showroom Internationale in Las Vegas for half the scheduled month by the day of the opening show. At $15 a head, two shows a day, seven days a week, that's nearly a million dollars in advance sales. Some meal ticket!

When the Colonel took El from Sun Records of Memphis to RCA Victor with the rights to all his material, issued and unissued, it didn't cost Victor more than $30,000 (plus a Cadillac for Presley himself). That's what good management can do for you.

What it can't do for you is give you talent, or even develop it like Sam Phillips did. Everyone knows about the Colonel, who masterminded the most profitable part of Presley's career but less is known of Phillips, the man responsible for the most creative part of his career, the record dealer who met this High School kid who wanted to cut a disc for his mom's birthday, tutored him for a year and a half, exposing him to the black music Phillips was selling on his Sun record label, and turning him into that eventual hit-maker.

Like most of the white kids round Tennessee and Missippi, Presley wanted to be a cowboy singer, though in later years El claimed a deep-founded liking for black music, claiming that he used to brave the displeasure of Vernon, his father, to listen to bluesmen like Arthur Crudup and Big Bill Broonzy. To compensate for liking sinful stuff like that, Presley used to take his guitar along to revivalist camp meetings to sing hymns, but that, too might be fantasy. 'His Hand in Mine'! Dunno. Presley marks the point where hagiography and discography get involved with each other never again to be disentagled, where the myth begins to become the reality.

If, as Elvis claims, he learnt so much from Arthur Crudup personally, then why did the old boy get not a cent from 'That's Alright', Crudup's song which was his first release for Sun? In fact, it was a cowboy song he did first, but it was so terrible Phillips never released it.

Perhaps this lack of tangible recognition is because, as reinterpreted by Presley, Crudup's song has been made peculiarly his own. Crudup's is a song of tragic resignation, the man whose chick has left him and what can he do but accept it? The shrug of the shoulders. Life goes on, goddammit, that's the real trouble. So: *'That's alright, momma'*.

Presley sings it defiantly. OK, so you want to split. That's your pleasure. Plenty more chicks where you came from. *'That's alright, momma'*. A different tempo. A different mood. Damn near a different melody.

Funny thing is, on his last British tour Crudup was doing *two* songs with similar words and one of them sounded like Presley's version. The other was the slower, fatalistic song, much as he recorded it so long ago, along with 'Death Valley Blues' and similar songs of stark and bitter resignation.

Folksong scholars are familiar with the phenomenon of traditional musicians learning songs back from collectors, but usually they are different songs. This could be one of the few times a singer has learned his own song back, so changed he himself accepts it as a thing new in its own right. Crudup is still too uptight to discuss the thing rationally, so we may never know if this is what happened, or if in fact he's always had two versions, but only recorded one, teaching the other to El.

Since 'That's Alright' there's been no real development in Presley, only degeneration. The aggressive defiance that transformed Carl Perkins' almost apologetic 'Blue Suede Shoes' and made it into a million seller is still there, though it is Presley reviving it and calling himself up like an ancestral god, the superstar in instant recall. This is what it was like.

(Not so, in fact. He now sings 'Blue Suede Shoes' about twice as fast as on the record. But, with all the shit that's come down since 1955, he's got to do it that way so it'll sound authentic. All the old rockers have to do the same: the singing is more frenzied, the gyrations more sexual, so that in today's mock-permissiveness they can seem as shocking as we remember them, back in the Nineteen Fifties.)

This must have been what it was like, why Ed Sullivan refused to have him on his TV show unless he wore a tuxedo, and kept the cameras trained exclusively upon the upper part of his body so the family audience could be spared the shock of Presley's crotch and hip movements, the strippers' bumps and grinds serving notice that man was returning to the mating dance of the peacock's rutting strut, and woman better pay attention and make her choice. The end of patriarchal society signalled by a rock singer's hips. Man the hunter becomes the hunted. Women's Lib makes man the sex object!

No wonder Sullivan stood at the side of the set muttering to himself 'Sonofabitch. Sonofabitch...' Whether he was impressed with the Presley charisma or horrified with disgust at what was described as its obscenity, there is no record, and this late, Sullivan's not telling.

This is what Presley was and this is what he is, despite the self-parody, despite his aging audience, of a piece with the nickleodeon one-arm banditry of Vegas, reminding them of their youth, at fifteen bucks the plate and cheap at the price. Most of the old records are still available, dating back to the Sun masters RCA bought in the Fifties, and the fans have them for comparison, so the live performances have to be an instant action replay of the records he made so long ago. Already, he has found a sort of immortality.

What Col Parker and the movie moguls of Paramount and MGM made of Presley was something else. They made him safe for the coach trade, doing what Tom Jones did later but that was all he had, coming on with sex but dropping the salacious mask of Dionysus at the very last moment, so you can see he's only kidding, really. The all-round entertainer. 'Love Me Tender'.

We know about sex and we've read all the manuals about the orgasms we ought to have been having and we're not, and it worries our minds in the midnight hour and then dear old Pres or Tom the Jones does his butch physical thing and we laugh like you do in a horror movie when you're really scared. If that is what it's really like, that funky stuff, and the sweat glistening on the upper lip, the bulging codpiece pants, the greaseball hair, nothing at all like Wilbur on his once-a-weak-is-enough five minute epics, then what am I doing married to this creep?

Then suddenly it's all a put-on, and the sickly sentimental ballad lets us in on the joke and he's our old friend the bar-room tenor:

'*Wi-i-i-ise men se-a-a-eh*
Only foo-oo-ools rush in
But I ... (but I ... but I)
Can't he'p
Falling in lu-ur-ve with ye-oo-w.'

Bet your life Wilbur could sing just like that, if he had the practice.

This is what they've taught him and he does it kind of well because the man (no boy, now) has talent, and anyway this is of a piece with the cowboy songs he used to dig back in Tupelo, Miss. But there is nothing in this sentimental schlock vein that hasn't been done, couldn't be done, wouldn't be done by Pat Boone and Steve Lawrence and Andy Williams (who's doing it still).

The real Elvis Presley, arrogant, defiant, triumphant, was the sound of Sam Phillips' Sun, backed up by Scotty Moore's country rock guitar and Bill Black's bass. This is what RCA-Victor Artistes and Repertoire man Steve Scholes heard at the Miami djs' convention and this is what he bought for his thirty thousand bucks, and some of his first issues diverted so little from it that they must have been unissued Sun masters sold as part of the deal. Scholes put Nashville guitar man Chet Atkins on to producing the new records, a smooth, technically proficient guitar picker to be sure, hot enough on his axe to have a particular lick named after him, but someone as far removed from Presley's teenage hot-pants image as Nashville is from Memphis in geography and spirit. Today the majors go down to Memphis to record Lulu and Dusty and Petula with that elusive sound they can't seem to get anywhere else, and Nashville has pulled itself out of the hole dug in the sand by its own, self-indulgent, maudlin tears, but in those days what they were trying to do was make Presley as bland as Atkins' metronomic, undemanding guitar-picking, and by gosh they succeeded. Presley for the mass market. Sex that all the family can enjoy. Amaze your friends. Be first on your block to have one. A literal mind-fucker.

By industry standards, these were quite well-written songs. Moon rhymed with June in the expected places. None of that stuff about hound-dogs and heartbreak hotels and be-bop-a-lula gibberish that sounded so crazy when Steve Allen used to read it out deadpan, like Shakespearian blank verse, on his programme. As the Vogue critic, Richard Goldstein, pointed out in his somewhat pretentious 'The Poetry of Rock', rock music lyrics are illiterate because that's what they're meant to be. The word, actually is unliterate: oral culture, music for the electronic village. None of that stuff in Presley's ballads.

So he became two people. One would rather switch than fight, but the other was the rebel who seemed to the grown-ups to be without any cause worth fighting for, when the cause was as simple as the newly-antlered stag challenging the king of the deer forest to come out and get licked, a personalized generation gap suggesting unmentionable inadequacies in the old stag's sexual equipment.

The trick was, to make the challenge apparent only to the rest of the challengers, not to the challenged. While the young studs cinched in their belts to show off their narrow arses and had their trousers cut tighter round the balls, while the young does wiggled their shoulders in delicious anticipation, the grown-ups could say to each other: Hot damn, that Presley guy can really sing if he wants to. Pity he doesn't drop all that 'uh-huh' stuff and develop his talents.

It was a great trick while it lasted, and after they got

to work on him, adding a vocal group and heavying up the beat of the up-tempo numbers, he notched up successes he couldn't have made with the little Memphis company. According to Charlie Gillett, he had the best-selling record for more than half the first two years he was with RCA – 55 weeks out of 104. He had 15 records in the Top Ten between 1955 and 1959 and 22 in the rhythm and blues Top Ten which in a way was more difficult, because there he was directly up against a lot of black competition.

Though today he sings songs like McCartney's 'Yesterday' in cabaret, he can rightly claim to have outsold all the singers who capitalized upon his desertion of country rock, like the Beatles, or who learnt from it and emulated it, like Tom Jones. Over 50 gold singles and 14 gold albums (at the last count) is a tough score to equal, leave alone beat.

Recited like that, it seems pretty impressive, but it conceals the dreary doldrums that came so soon after he left Memphis, a gap which was filled by Little Richard and, for a while, by Sam Phillips' next discovery, the Richard-influenced white piano player, Jerry Lee Lewis. It was into that doldrums that the four lads from Liverpool leapt in 1962 – and it's instructive to note that the first successes of the Beatles date from the period when Presley stopped appearing in public. But that is a later story.

Sinatra and Presley have this in common: between them they mark the end of the star era and the birth of the superstar era. The crooner used the outdated techniques of mechanized big-band swing to sing for and to the first of the new generation. The white rock 'n' roller used the new forms, but under the influence of the industry was persuaded to sing more and more for the older generations. But while Sinatra developed new styles to handle the different stages of his career, by the time of Presley, old-style pop singing was so moribund that there was nothing fresh he could do with it. Pretty soon they were all doing

Lennon-McCartney songs to prove they were with it. And the growth of black music in popularity meant that there was less scope for singers like Haley and Presley who imitated black styles unless, like the Beatles, they were able to add something uniquely their own.

The result is that, with a few exceptions, as a rock singer Presley has produced hardly anything fresh since the mid-Fifties. 'Guitar Man', with its witty lyrics about a rock musician looking for work and eventually finding it, enlivened with the lively picking of the composer (first of Presley's back-up guitarists to stand comparison with Scotty Moore, though the touch is actually lighter than that of the old Memphis guitar man), is the only one that comes to mind. 'In the Ghetto', with its patronizing white liberal sanctimoniousness, stands out as the nadir, not merely because we suspect it of insincerity: in drinking deep of the seminal fountain of black eroticism, Presley had paid a much profounder compliment to the Afro-American, acknowledging implicity at the same time that American society owes more to black people than just their music.

And so Presley became acceptable to the mass media. Pressmen who have raged at the obscenity of his movements queued in line to praise what he was doing at the Showroom Internationale. TV made him the subject of a spectacular feature programme, with his name spelt out in lightbulbs, and a special section paying tribute to black music leading up to 'In the Ghetto'.

Typically, it was too late. Jack Good's TV spectaculars had done it all before, and Mike Wadleigh's 'Woodstock' had turned the cameras to where the action really was, with the skinny dipping in the muddy water, the joint burning, the fucking in the long grass, while Grace Slick called from the stage for volunteers for a revolution.

Meanwhile, the king was at Las Vegas. And Col Parker sure looked happy.

IV

A Word of Explanation for Mr. Jones

*"The leaders of the Now revolution hold nightly
court in the discotheques, but in Carnaby Street
the revolution is . . . right here . . . in the bright
sunlight of a smoky London day the main body
of the revolution pass and repass, codifying the
visual legislation of their declaration of intent
in today . . ."*

*"Basically, the story began as long ago as 1944,
when Mr. R. A. Butler's Education Act gave
the bulk of the population access to the wonder-
land of real knowledge for the first time ever:
calculus . . . Picasso . . . words . . . ideas . . .
pictures! Three years later the soldiers came
home, with an explosive result which now means
that there are over two million hard-earning
people between 15 and 19 years old."*

–Swinging London, 1967

I ACTUALLY know the Mr Jones in Bob Dylan's 'Ballad of
a Thin Man'. He's a good friend of mine who spent a lot
of time interviewing the singer during the big 1965 tour
and though the song is unfair to him, I'm sure Dylan is
right. I'm sure he really doesn't understand what's
happening, however hard he tries.

But he does try. He doesn't come on as if he knew it
all before Robert Zimmerman left Minnesota for the big
city, he doesn't try to make over each new talent into his
own image of what pop art should be, as if nothing had
happened since 1950, as if the whole basis of all art hadn't
changed in the past two decades, he doesn't patronise
the new kinds in the hopes that everything that happens
now will turn out to be only new variations on everything

that happened way back then, remember when.

My favourite show biz character is Dick Rowe of Decca, who turned down the Beatles, and let them go to EMI. I prefer him, actually, to George Martin, who signed them, somewhat reluctantly, because Martin and Dick James, who did young Lennon and McCartney the enormous favour of publishing their songs for them, stumbled across the genius of the Sixties by accident, even though they have been complimenting themselves on their cleverness in being right there ever since. In rejecting what he heard, Rowe was truer to the old principles of show biz.

He was right: the Beatles negated everything he believed in, the whole Denmark Street-Albert Embankment business aesthetic, by which rock 'n' roll was to be only a temporary phenomenon, a minor aberration. Normal service will be resumed immediately.

When they told Brian Epstein in 1962 that groups with guitars were on the way out, Decca were merely echoing the show biz orthodoxy which had been trying to kill rock 'n' roll since the mid-Fifties – not so much because they disliked it, because to be perfectly honest there was very little in popular music which they could swear, hand on heart, they really enjoyed at all. But that was the way pop music was, a series of inexplicable in-and-out fads, wasn't it? I mean, the idea that 20 years later Elvis would be still singing 'Hound Dog' on prime-time TV, was just plain ludicrous.

So, hard on the heels of Presley's 'All Shook Up' in 1956, Victor and Columbia were busily promoting calypso as a new craze to succeed rock 'n' roll for a short while until they thought of something better. After all, it had all the superficially similar characteristics that had made the kids take rock to their bosoms: it was black in origin, with a nice semi-Latin beat to it (something the show-biz tycoons found it easier to relate to than the relentless four-in-the-bar beat of hard rock), and more emphasis upon the words. A fillip for sheet music sales!

There was a thing in Britain called skiffle, of course, a strange hybrid of thumping knees-up-mother-Brown beat and black prison songs, but that was bound to die. It had happened by accident, in January 1956, when 'Rock Island Line' sold 300,000 copies after only two airplays. It was so accidental, the singer who made the hit got only his £10 session fee out of it, though it made him a star. Skiffle had many of the superficial characteristics of rock plus one additional disadvantage – it was self-evidently a home-made music, a true people's art, as rough round the edges and unself-consciously inartistic as the doggerel jingles strikers had sung in 1926.

Consequently, though they continued to make pots of money out of the three-chord kids who were willing to adopt a nasal twang and play the night away with wash-board and tea-chest bass for all the espresso coffee you could drink and possibly a few bob for the fare home on the night bus (just possibly), the show biz establishment hated skiffle. Not merely the true-to-caricature cigar-chomping managers and agents, but also the Musicians' Union officials who were equally part of the way the game had come to be played.

When I debated the significance of skiffle with the MU's card-carrying CPer assistant secretary at one of those futile public confrontations beloved of the polemicists of the neo-Stalinist left in 1956, the air was thick with racist talk of 'jungle music'. The Africa within!

But skiffle could be expected to die. The thing was calypso, and Belafonte's 'Mary's Boy Child' occupying the traditional White Christmas spot at number one right through into the beginning of 1958 kind of clinched it. Nancy Whiskey's skiffle-styled 'Freight Train' selling a million copies didn't change the pattern, for the really important sellers, besides calypso, were once again the ballad singers – Guy Mitchell, Frankie Vaughan, Tab Hunter, Andy Williams, Perry Como, Michael Holliday. Rock itself (or the music that got labelled rock: though

they were great for the categories game, the show biz
bosses chose what they applied the labels to in ways that
only they could explain, and probably not even they) was
getting sweeter. Singers like Paul Anka (who later wrote
'My Way' for Sinatra) could be passed off as rock since
their material was clearly teen-exploitation of a fairly
obvious sort, though they were really closer to the
older-style crooners, as Charlie Gillett has pointed out.
Presley even was getting sweeter, too, with 'Love Me
Tender', 'It's Now or Never', 'Are You Lonesome
Tonight?', and 'Wooden Heart'.

Skiffle intruded only occasionally into all this sweetness
and light, though at a grassroots level it was running right
across the gardens of popular music like an uncontrollable
weed. There were reported to be 600 skiffle clubs in
London, and even the dozy old BBC had to start a
Saturday morning show to canalize all the talent into safe
directions. But the show biz establishment knew it was
bound to die, even if it took an unconscionable long time
doing it. A good job for them they didn't hold their breaths
waiting, for before 1956 was out John Lennon and his
mates at Quarry Bank High School were playing skiffle for
pennies around Liverpool.

Not that it was personalities who were making the
change. They could be easily absorbed, as Lonnie Donegan's
metamorphosis from skiffler into variety comic singer
showed. It was really as simple as the birth-rate statistics.
Since counting heads was their trip (a political heads and
tails they call democracy), it's surprising, really, that they
failed to suss what was happening.

By 1956, the great year of rock 'n' roll, the teenage
explosion had really started: there were 24 million
American kids between 10 and 20 in 1955 and there are
nearly twice as many now (not counting those who have
been culled in Vietnam). But population doesn't tell you
everything.

The man came home after 1914–18 as well, and they

were welcomed into bed just as warmly by their wives. Only when *their* kids left school they joined the breadline. Ten years after the end of World War I the Stock Market crashed and a world-wide depression started that only another world war could cure. Unemployment in USA rose in the four years after the crash from $1\frac{1}{2}$ million in 1929 to nearly 13 million in 1933. In Britain it had been over a million since 1925 and it kept rising until the outbreak of war.

By 1955 it was down to just 170,000, an eighth of the 1938 figure. The people had more money, too. In USA, they had half as much more to spend in real terms than they'd had in 1929. That's everyone: men, women, kids, senile aged, teenyboppers, all. The kids had even more, proportionately, especially those of proletarian origins. In Britain, for instance, the working class share of the country's total income had risen from 45 per cent in 1938 to 54 per cent in 1954.

It was a few years before the merchants woke up to the potential market represented by all these extra young people with money jingling in their pockets. By 1959, the London Press Exchange ad agency had commissioned Mark Abrams to find how much the kids had to spend. He made it official. According to his reckoning, British teenagers had twice as much buying power than they'd had twenty years before: a cool nine hundred million!

In a year, their spending on records rose from £15 million to £17 million. Not only that: they bought nearly half the discs sold. Small wonder record sales soared. The US teen population doubled between 1955 and today. So did record sales. Coincidence? No: teenage power!

Abrams said something significant in 1959 that began to come true almost immediately: 'The aesthetic of the teenage market is essentially a working class aesthetic and probably only entrepreneurs of working class origin will have a natural understanding of the needs of the market.'

Meanwhile, the electronic revolution was getting going,

D

too. In 1925 there'd been two million radio sets in Britain. In 1947 there'd been only 14,000 TV licenses and in the four years that followed they'd just reached three-quarters of a million. By five years later, in September 1956, the figure was six million. Another million had been added by April 1957, and it became eight million only a few weeks later. A hyperbolic curve.

But this is a less significant statistic than it seems. The real generation gap was opening up between the older people, 80 per cent of them staying home hypnotized by the gogglebox five nights or more a week, and the kids ranging round town, a transistor radio slung by a strap from their wrists like a walkie-talkie. The teenagers were mobile!

During the 1950s I went to a dance at the Sporthalle in East Berlin. Half the kids in the audience ignored the boring, old-fashioned, official band and grooved on rock 'n' roll coming from transistors pressed to their ears. Later that night I saw the same leather-jacketed halb-starke kids chorusing Pete Seeger protest songs louder than the Party functionaries who'd failed to keep them out of the official reception for a British singer over on a visit. I know: I was that singer.

The same set of contradictions were sharpening between the kids and the aging bureaucrats all over the industrialized world: in New York, London, Paris, West Berlin, East Berlin, Prague. Old labels yellowed and peeled off. The industrial age was ending, and the two sides who'd had such a fight back in the 1890s about who would control the game had to unite to fight this new menace, these educated kids with an electric, working class, revolutionary aesthetic who weren't even interested in seizing power. (Only in one country, China, did the bosses of the ruling power structure have the wit to sense that the only way to head off the kids from shattering the state completely was to march on ahead of them down a blind alley: so for a time power went out to the streets. But only for a time. Then they sicced the army on to the people.)

The kids were beginning to realize that they were growing into a world that had no room for them. Norbert Wiener, founder of the science of cybernetics, compared the output of most mass media in 1950 to 'a standardized inoffensive and insignificant product which, like the white bread of the bakeries, is made rather for its keeping and selling properties than for its food value'. The real problem, he wrote, was to find 'colorable material' for the intellectual proletarians pouring out of higher education establishments to work upon.

'This is fundamentally an external handicap of modern communications,' he wrote, 'but it is paralleled by another which gnaws from within. This is the cancer of creative narrowness and feebleness.'

Wiener was right about the impetus towards trivia. Writing before the LP had made its full impact upon the mass media, his pessimism was understandable. But professional intellectuals like Richard Hoggart (the title of his book, 'The Uses of Literacy', tells where *he* is at) could only view the future with the same pessimism seven years later, though the situation had changed radically: '... genuine class culture is being eroded in favour of the mass opinion, the mass recreational product, and the generalized emotional response. The world of club-singing is being gradually replaced by that of typical radio dance-music and crooning, television cabaret and commercial-radio variety. The uniform national type which the popular papers help to produce is writ even larger in the uniform international type which the film-studios of Hollywood present. The old forms of class culture are in danger of being replaced by a poorer kind of classless, or by what I was led earlier to describe as a 'faceless', culture, and this is to be regretted.'

It is typical that all along, Hoggart writes of media that are already obsolescent. This was published in 1957 and perhaps he had passed the proofs before the growth of skiffle had begun the counter-trend. But the same gloomy judgement was retained when the book was reprinted in 1968, the year which is to the youth revolution what 1848 was to the equally unsuccessful revolutionaries of the Nineteenth Century.

BE A REALIST: DEMAND THE IMPOSSIBLE! (Paris student graffiti, May 1968).

LET'S OPEN THE GATES OF NURSERIES, UNIVERSITIES, AND OTHER PRISONS! (Nanterre, 1968).

IMAGINATION IS SEIZING POWER! (Sorbonne, 1968).

WE ARE THE WRITING ON YOUR WALL! (London Street Commune, 1969).

Frantz Fanon described how during the Algerian liberation struggle transistor radios united the people with the rebels fighting the French: 'Traditional resistances broke down and one could see in a *douar* groups of families in which fathers, mothers, daughters, elbow to elbow, would scrutinize the radio dial, waiting for Voice of Algeria.' The little radios had the same unifying and liberating effect on the kids.

When the BBC refused to play records from anyone outside the big EMI-Decca combines on the radio, the independent producers bought time on the pirate commercial radios to promote their products, producing the greatest flowering in British pop since the beginnings of rock. Though the businessman's Labour government sank the pirates, their programme techniques and some of their talent was taken over lock-stock-and-fab-forty by the BBC's 'official' pirate station, Radio One.

Anthropologists have pointed out that primitive peoples are often more at home with modern technology than university-trained literates. Hopi Indians find it quite easy to understand Einsteinian physics, according to Bernard Lee Whorf, simply *because* they can't read or write. The Chinese cultural revolution, though officially inspired, expressed itself like the Paris of May 1968 in graffiti: big character posters using the total-concept ideograms of ancient China, as applicable to the electronic utopia and to the past as the I Ching, the ancient book of changes. Meanwhile, as part of his industrialization programme, Mao was trying to get them to use Western-style linear one-letter-at-a-time printing. Too late!

Meanwhile, with look-and-say techniques, English teachers are trying to make words back into ideograms in which each word is a total shape, rather than the collection of phonetic sound symbols they have become. The educationalist reactionaries are right: they're threatening the whole structure of our schools system, constructed so carefully in 1870 to produce workers just literate enough to work the new machines.

All this is pretty straight-forward McLuhanism, except that, like most of his generation, McLuhan has tended to over-value the impact of TV on the kids, though it has affected their parents very profoundly, making their social institutions obsolete *for them*.

Time magazine reported on what happened after the shooting of Bobby Kennedy: 'On that first awful morning last week, many Americans phoned relatives and friends; unable to speak the unspeakable, they just said "Turn on the television". Thus began a four-day period in which TV and radio attempted to link a distraught country into a comprehending whole. They succeeded to a remarkable degree.'

Pete Seeger once suggested to me that local radio stations (in America, where the FM stations, in particular, can have more independence, politically) ought to broadcast protest songs on demonstration days to get everyone singing the same song at the same time all along an entire march.

Typical white-liberal-Marxist thinking. What radios ought to do is to get everyone singing *different* songs at the same time. Electronics encourage diversity, compared with the uniformity of print. That's their merit, and why highly institutionalized media like most TV stations and big newspapers and periodicals (and even some underground papers today), and radio in countries like Britain and France and the Soviet Union where an industrial-bureaucratic dictatorship rules, have had such small impact on the kids, despite the suitability of their forms. As Marx realized, the control of the means of production is as vital as the form – and communications are the essential means of production which are revolutionizing society today.

When they finally get round to hooking up the TV videotape libraries with computerized access through dialling-in systems, when the different TV tape cassette systems are made compatible, then the organization of the mass media will finally have to catch up with the artistic needs created by the technology. Resist it as they will undoubtedly try, they will not be able to ignore the kids' same feedback response to the product that they now have to records by way of the shops. And as soon as they are allowed to see what they want whenever they want, the kids will start watching, preferably on portables.

When a voting button is incorporated, making possible instant plebiscites, everyone will become the government, an idea they tried to implement in Paris in 1792, only they didn't have the right hardware then (the most potent medium for reaching the masses was the street ballad, which was allowed into the French National Convention until Danton got the ballad singers chucked out on March 16, 1794). Once the hardware exists, the kids will take over politics. And abolish it, along with its divide-and-rule star system.

Meanwhile, they are changing things where they have the power. To try to understand the Beatles and Dylan without realizing that they are using the star system's techniques to smash the star system is to fail completely to understand what is happening.

Isn't it, Mr Jones?

WE ARE THE
WRITING ON
YOUR WALL

24,000,000 × 2
imaginat (1971)
ion is seizin g
power

American
KIDS
between
10 years
20 years &
24,000,000
(1955)

Today was Yesterday

"So I thought, well let's put them under contract. I can't lose much".

–George Martin

THE BEATLES were a con, the clean-washed dream of an unhappy petit-bourgeois Jewish gay boy called Brian Epstein who was killed by the con in the end. This is the basic, unpalateable, incontrovertible fact about them that the show biz establishment has not yet digested, though they've been told it often enough, and by the four Beatles themselves.

When John Lennon said 'We have a today image' every-one believed him and missed the irony, including the *Daily Mirror,* who revelled in 'the nutty, noisy, happy, hand-some Beatles' and explained that they might 'wear their hair like a mop – but it's WASHED, it's super clean. So is their fresh young act'. That was Brian Epstein, not the Beatles they were writing about.

As John Lennon wrote in his joke biography of the Beatles in the pre-Epstein, pre-EMI, pre-George Martin, pre-MBE days of July 1961: 'And then a man with a beard cut off said – will you go to Germany (Hamburg) and play mighty rock for the peasants for money? And we said we would play mighty anything for money.'

They chose the name Beatles when they were in Hamburg because the way it's pronounced in German it sounds like a little boy's rude word for his cock: Peedles. That was when they were leather-jacketed rockers, playing for eight hours at a stretch bombed out of their heads on beer and slimming pills, getting deported when they set light to their sleeping quarters in the Bambi cinema.

'There has been a lot of publicity and there will be more and in this connection it will be of vital importance to live up to the publicity. Note that on ALL the above engagements during the performances, smoking, eating, chewing and drinking is STRICTLY PROHIBITED, *prohibited.*'

That was Brian Epstein in 1962.

'So suddenly all back in Liverpool village were many groups playing in grey suits and Jim said "Why have you no grey suits?" "We don't like them, Jim," we said speaking to Jim.'

That was John Lennon in 1961.

But Brian and Paul McCartney between them put the Beatles into suits. Paul said in the film of 'Let It Be': 'Mr Epstein said, sort of "get suits on" and we did. And so we were always fighting that discipline a bit.' Later, Lennon was to say that the Beatles began to sell out right then, but really what they were doing was attempting to use the enemy's weapons to knock him out. That's when the con started. The suits, and the MBEs in 1965 showed how far they were going to have to go to keep the con going, even though they refused to do any more Royal Variety Performances after the first one in 1963.

As Edward Heath said, they were the salvation of the corduroy industry. Brian Epstein threatened to sue schmutte firms who made short bum-freezer jackets without lapels and collars and called them Beatle jackets — unless they paid a royalty to him. Girls started wearing acrylic Beatle wigs. Writers in the men's fashion press complained that the so-called Beatle jacket had been designed by Pierre Cardin in the first place anyway.

Soon the argument became academic. Though Dora Bryan took over the White Christmas chart slot with a song whose only merit was the word Beatle in the title, the clothing industry was discovering that for some reason you couldn't sell any old junk with a Beatle tag (the commercial jargon is 'character merchandise') the way you could package up Donald Duck's grin or James Bond's Luger. Later Bob Dylan warned: 'Don't follow leaders.' The kids were already not doing it. Firms went out of business with warehouses full of the bum-freezer suits.

The con. It required a sort of brilliance, the ability to put together all the second-hand musical cliches of previous pop (including the Glenn Miller major sixth at the end of 'She Loves You', for instance) and end up with something of their own. But at all costs the real, the essential individual identities must be suppressed in favour of a Beatles, today image.

Beatles couldn't write poems like:

'I remember a time when
Everybody I loved hated me
Because I hated them.
So what, so what, so
Fucking what.

'I remember a time when
Belly buttons were knee high
When only shitting was
Dirty and everything else
Clean and beautiful.'

That had to wait until 'Working Class Hero' got banned in Britain and America, though the poem was written by John Lennon in a letter to Stu Sutcliffe in 1961. Pre-Epstein.

The con grew out of their experience of the show biz bureaucracy and the way things worked inside those little pointed heads full of pound and dollar signs. They learnt from their know-it-all know-nothing approach to pop. They learnt it hard, and carefully.

They learnt it from Decca and the bad advice they'd received from Brian before the audition, to ignore their own songs and stick to standards. George Harrison sang 'The Sheik of Araby'. Paul sang 'Red Sails in the Sunset'. Then it was Don't call us: we'll call you. The whole bit.

They learnt it from George Martin, A&R man at one of EMI's less successful companies, Parlophone, the man who'd done fine recording Bob and Alf Pearson ('my brother and I'), the Five Smith Brothers ('Hello hello hello hello *hello-o-o!* Mr and Mrs Smith's five little boys...are singing to *you*...') and of course Jimmy Shand ('Bluebell Polka', still selling) but was out of his depth with rock 'n' roll. The man who dug Peters Ustinov and Sellers, but he turned down Tommy Steele when he was plain Tommy Hicks, the sailorboy on leave playing his skiffle at the Two I's, the man looking for another Cliff Richard and the Shadows (there is a little bit of Dick Rowe in all of us). He wasn't about to make the same mistake twice. Better signed than sorry.

'When I first met them I'd already heard a tape that they'd done that frankly wasn't very impressive. It had bad sound on it and the songs weren't very impressive. I don't think they were actually Beatle compositions' (you mean he can't actually *remember*?) 'but there was something about it that I thought was rather interesting so I thought well let's get them down to the studio and have a look at them. And I was immediately impressed by them as people, not by them as musicians. I liked them. They were most engaging people. They had that kind of irreverent sense of humour that I also nursed. And I thought they were super people to be with. And incidentally I thought that they sang in a very engaging and very unusual style also.

So I thought, well, let's put them under contract. I can't lose much. And that was the beginning of them.'

Correction. That was the beginning of how George Martin and his show biz buddies remember them, back in the days when he earned less than eight quid a week. The beginning had been long before, when Pete Best joined the band to play drums and they went to Hamburg in 1960, Pete laying down the simple basic beat which is now Ringo's hallmark. They paid their dues, not only in Hamburg and Liverpool, but also in scruffy dancehall hops all over Britain, playing second to a local band or a big star from London, building up a mass following the hard way in the months between December 1961 when Decca turned them down and September 1962 when they recorded 'Love Me Do' with George Martin. He'd signed them in June but he still kept looking for his Cliff and the Shadows, or even a Cliff to put in front of the Beatles. In the end he gave up and recorded them anyway.

During that time I was touring the country with Smart's Circus, running a team of men in yellow and orange vans sticking bills all over the trees and walls of beautiful Britain, and I noticed this crazy name on the posters we were covering up, getting bigger and bigger, climbing from 'and also' to 'special attraction' to 'and featuring' until they were top, in caps right across the quad crowns: THE BEATLES!

If Martin hadn't recorded them then, someone else would have discovered them. Hell, I was already wondering who they were myself, their following seemed to be growing so steadily wherever we went! If I'd been into rock then (I hated it) I might have done something about it.

What they learnt from George Martin was that though they had to rely upon themselves, the business was run by so many berks, it was possible to please them, to give them what they thought they wanted, without too much difficulty. Conquest from within.

After 'Love Me Do' got to number 17, Martin offered them as a follow-up 'How Do You Do It?', a song he'd got from a so far not-very-successful crooner-turned-music publisher called Dick James whose single big success had been the main title music for the 'Robin Hood' TV series. George Martin had recorded it (and it spawned a host of kids' folklore parodies from Liverpool to Sydney, incidentally).

The Beatles sussed that this song wasn't really for them, although in return for the favour of taking 'How Do You Do It?' James had agreed to publish their songs, which was a pretty magnaminious gesture on his part, considering the low level of lyrics your average rock group was turning out those days. But they still said no.

Martin got really angry at this petulant show of independence from a group whose lousy songs couldn't get above number 17. Why, 'Robin Hood' got to number nine. If they were determined to turn down a hit, they'd have to produce something just as good. They went away and came back with 'Please Please Me'. A palpable hit, in terms he could understand. He'd taught them a formula.

This, more than anything else, was what made the Beatles so successful. Like another great songwriting talent of the period, Lionel Bart, they had a genius for pastiche, the ability to make songs that sounded like something you'd heard on the car radio the day before but forgotten. Faced with nothing schlock like 'How Do You Do It?' they said fine, OK, you want nothing schlock, we can do nothing schlock ('and we said we would play mighty anything for money'), and they produced a song that was the quintessence of nothing schlock, triple distilled and aged in the wood, an instant hit, full of Sam Goldwyn-type new cliches, words of one syllable telling simple, basic truths that were closer to what it was like to be a teenager in Conservative Britain than any of the American teen-exploitation songs had been to *their* kids.

Musically, they weren't so original. Their vocal har

monies owed a lot to the Everly Brothers. Their approach to their instruments was similarly inspired by Chuck Berry. Despite the pretentiousness of William Mann's analysis in *The Times,* then an even greater gesture from the establishment than their MBEs, their melodies were not as original as all that. The 'pandiatonic clusters' which caught his ear so forcefully in 'That Boy' probably derived from the fact that they were writing their tunes on the white notes of the piano; if they composed 'Not a Second Time' in the key of A, that would account for the 'Aeolian cadence' at the end, not the influence of Mahler's 'Das Lied von der Erde', because if you play A to A on the white notes of the piano, what comes out is what musicologists call the Aeolian mode, an antique scale which is used in so many English folk songs, though, strangely not many to be heard around Liverpool which tend to be simple Ionian major scales.

Their vocal attack was something else, with roots, perhaps, in folk. Liverpool is one of those towns where it's always been OK to sing a local folk song like 'Maggy May' without sounding twee. Even my own Geordie-land, with its inflated idea of its cultural importance, doesn't sing 'Blaydon Races' in quite so unself-conscious a manner. The Beatles' vocal attack, which came from a Scouse trying to sing Spade, a strained upper-register thing that generated excitement of a particularly . . . English *provincial* kind . . . set pop on a new direction that carried it over a watershed on to a whole new vocal trip.

Ewan MacColl has pointed out that, until the Beatles, most pop singing styles were merely art song in developing stages of degeneration, regressing by way of light opera and musical comedy to the 1930–1940 crooner, whose main contribution was to allow the amplifying powers of the microphone to invest his voice with more interest than it really had, bringing out the softer, breathier, boudoire tones of his voice. But MacColl, a folk singer whose sharp perceptions seem to desert him as soon as he comes close to electric instruments, has not pursued his analysis into the contemporary scene, possibly because a careful look at modern pop would force him to abandon his so carefully nurtured liberal-Marxist paternal attitudes to 'music of the people' (he comes on these days like a Maoist, politically, but much of what he has to say aesthetically is pure Hampstead Left Book Club intellectual, circa 1938).

What made pre-and post-Beatles pop singing so different from each other was the attempt to sing in a black manner. It had been tried before, of course, but it is hardly surprising that the most successful attempt originated in Liverpool, cosmopolitan mixing-pot of the sea-ways. Blues singer Redd Sullivan, who worked for a while firing Cunarder boilers before he came into music by way of skiffle, once pointed out to me that the seamen who always tuned their radios to the nearest shore stations wherever they were at sea were exposed to so many different cultural influences that Nashville country music and Missippi blues could get right down into their blood, making blues or bluegrass quite natural music to hear in the Merseyside waterfront pubs, without any of the pretensions that drove so many middle class art students to take up de blues in the late Sixties. In the days before more powerful transmitters and receivers and more efficient records distribution were to turn the world into one great village, these matelots were dreaming the future.

It started even before the invention of radio, for the last halfway successful amalgam between black and white musics also involved Liverpool – in the brief days of the clipper ships, that period between the end of the war of 1812 and the opening of the Suez Canal, when Englishmen needed worksongs to help them raise the anchor and attend to the rigging with extra speed, on thousand-mile journeys when every minute counted. It was a need they hadn't suffered, probably, since the very early prehistoric times. Not since the raising of Stonehenge, if indeed that was done by manual labour.

In a time of violent social change, then as now, the seamen found what they needed out of Africa, in the music taken to Haiti, the Guianas, Northern Brazil, the Caribbean and the United States by members of West African civilizations like the Ibo kingdom, smashed and decimated by the slavers. Sailors who scorned the Africans as black savages borrowed their call-and-response pattern of singing (eg: 'She loves you' 'Yeah yeah yeah') and much of the 'metronomic' rhythm that is such a feature of West African music to help them swing the work on.

The rhythm was the thing. A black prisoner called 'Bama told Alan Lomax that in the Missippi State Penitentiary at Parchman in 1947, and it didn't matter 'if he could sing just like Peter could preach and he didn't know what to sing about well he wouldn't do no good.

'Well here's a feller, maybe he ain't got no voice for singing but he been co-operating with the people so long and been on the job so long till he know just exactly how it should go and if he can just mostly talk it and you understand how to work, well it go good.

'The time, that's all it is. You can just whistle and if you know the time you can stay in time with the axe, you can whistle and you can cut just as well as if you were singing but you have to be experienced.'

The sailors put English words to the old African songs, some of them so scurrilous that anyone singing a sea shanty in Her Majesty's Royal Navy got the lash; Jack Tar worked to the tune of the unseditious fiddle.

The blacks borrowed the songs right back again – 'The Banana Boat Song' that was such a success for Belafonte in the calypso period after the first wave of rock 'n' roll had ebbed, that's a black song based on a salacious English sailor ditty called 'Little Sally Racket'.

The sea shanty flowered briefly as the industrial revolution poured black smoke over Englishmen on sea and land. Then it choked and quietened, as steam ships chugging through the Suez Canal replaced the great tea

E

clippers who'd raced to cut minutes off the journey from Foochow to London and get the best prices for their cargoes.

Black influences on English popular music persisted, though in sweeter, more palatable forms. In 1843 Whitlock's Virginia Minstrels visited Britain from USA, playing the polite, paternalistic versions of Afro-American plantation songs – especially those based on white originals – which were taken to heart by the middle class. Nigger minstrel troupes entertained at the end of every seaside pier; the publishers William and James Francis (of Francis, Day and Hunter) had a troupe before they opened up their music shop in Charing Cross Road.

There is something of this in the music of the Beatles. After all, the tune of 'Maggie May' comes from 'Old Folks at Home' (as does 'Keep Yer Feet Still, Geordie Hinnie' and 'Jesse James'). Purists who object to white Englishmen singing the blues prefer to ignore this.

The other thing which the Beatles had was a sort of ethnic humour, which Martin recognized as something he could relate to straight away, for laid over the strain of dry Merseyside scouse was the electronic Goonery of Peter Sellers and Spike Milligan (the 'Jim' in that early Beatles biography by John Lennon). As Dylan was learning at approximately the same time, they could bring it to bear upon the daft questions journalists asked, not so much because the questions were so daft themselves, as because they knew (like the Denmark Street tycoons) that this rubbish was what the punters wanted to know. So when they asked silly questions they got silly answers.

'What do you call that hairstyle?'

'Fred.'

'Why does Ringo wear so many rings on his fingers?'

'Because he can't get them through his nose.'

Though they were equally inaccessible to pretentious questions, if anyone wanted to talk about the music in terms that showed genuine interest, and weren't loaded down with academicist bullshit, he had their attention. So at their first New York news conference it was disc jockey Murray Kaufman, Murray the K, who knew something about their music and asked about it, rather than their haircuts, who earned their respect sufficiently to be made a sort of mascot for their tour, going everywhere with them, and eventually compering their enormous Shea Stadium concert for them.

After the Dick Lester movies they began to talk like characters out of an Alun Owen play. Owen had always had a good ear for the flat, dry, sardonic wit of Merseyside but wedded to the slick jump-cutting and pyxilated direction of Dick Lester, fresh from the thousand-pounds-a-puff world of making TV commercials, where the 30-second breaks can cost more than the hour-long musical spectacular before and the two-hour drama afterwards, the result had a strange artificality. Though later the Beatles said they hated what Dick Lester made of them, when they made their own movie, the rather disastrous 'Magical Mystery Tour', the visual debts were obvious.

And their very lifestyle owed a lot to Owen and Lester – from Owen they re-learnt their own dialogue and from Lester a way of life that leapt about from Savile Row to Katmandu in seconds. They were heroes of a drama someone was writing about four Liverpool boys who formed a beat group and made good, and starred in a drama about four Liverpool boys who formed a beat group and made good, and starred . . .

It was Pirandellian: '. . . *tho' she feels she's in a play She is anyway.*' (Penny Lane)

They used to pardoy their look-alike image, the creation of Brian Epstein. When Sir David Ormsby-Gore (now Lord Harlech, boss of Harlech TV) greeted John Lennon at the steps of the British Embassy in Washington DC, John replied: 'I'm not John. I'm Charlie. That's John.' And he pointed to George Harrison.

'Hello John,' said the ambassador.

'I'm not John,' said George, 'I'm Frank. That's John.' And he pointed to Paul.

As Ringo left, he asked the ambassador: 'And what do you do?'

By the time of Magical Mystery Tour it was becoming an obsession, though they had long discarded the look-alike gear. It became overlaid with the overtones of oriental mysticism during the Maharishi episode: *I am he as you are he as you are me and we are all together'* (I am the Walrus).

Later on they were to sing *'the walrus is Paul'* though we'd always thought they meant John Lennon, and John himself later confirmed it. ' "No you're not" cries Nicola, laughing at his funny feathery hat.' (from the film)

That was the year of Brian Epstein's death, of drugs and LSD, of Sgt Pepper, issued in July 1967 after four months' work (their first album took one day). At the time it seemed the most integrated, the most perfect rock record ever made (if you could indeed call it rock) but later, as the Lonely Hearts Club Band began to break up visibly, it could be seen that what was happening was four separate trips, not one joint tour.

The strain of those American tours had left them with something else besides sheer exhaustion. For a start, the simple rock of 'the nutty, noisy, happy, handsome Beatles' seemed to have already disappeared, sucked up by the monster crowds at the Shea Stadium and the Coliseum. Later it was to re-surface in songs like 'Lady Madonna' and 'Get Back', but as almost self-parody.

Though it came to us as an incredible flash of musical enlightenment, the total concept of 'Sgt Pepper' was really an expansion of what had already been said perfectly, in musical terms, in 'Strawberry Field Forever' and 'Penny Lane', while its message was more concisely and less ambiguously expressed in 'All You Need is Love', the song in Basic English written for the world TV spectacular seen by 150 million people.

That was the year of flower power, born in the San Francisco Human Be-In of January and ceremonially slaughtered on Haight-Ashbury on Friday October 6, with the burning of a coffin containing the stock schlock commercial hippie artifacts, the beads and the now almost meaningless nuclear disarmament runes and the pot pipes. Two days before, the Haight's Psychedelic Shop had closed its doors. July and 'All You Need is Love' seemed a million years behind already.

The four individual trips continued. George Harrison's 'Within You, Without You' on Pepper brought the sitar out from the backing role it had played on 'Norwegian Wood', was further developed on Mystery Tour by the mantra-like *'Please don't be long please don't be very long'* of 'Blue Jay Way' and by 'That Inner Light' on the back of the 'Lady Madonna' single.

Ringo's trip was closer to the folkie music hall tradition of Liverpool pubs like the Gregson's Wells where the Spinners still run a weekly singalong night in the room upstairs. This tradition is part of the Beatles' collective heritage – 'When I'm Sixty-Four' was based on an idea they were messing about with in the Cavern days, and Paul's 'Maxwell's Silver Hammer' had something of the same, with Mad magazine overtones. Of all four, however, Ringo seems to be striving least and to be most contented with where he is at right now, modest though his achievements might have been so far.

Paul's trip probably took its separate direction that day in Paris when he rushed into George Martin with a pretty tune he'd written, except the only words he could think of to go to it were 'Scrambled eggs'. He'd also thought of calling it 'Yesterday' but it sounded too corny. Martin persuaded him that, corny or not, 'Yesterday' was a good idea, and commercially he turned out to be right. According to Hunter Davies' 'authorized biography' of the Beatles, it's been their most recorded song. At the time of the book's publication (1968), it had been 'recorded by 119 different artists, ranging from Pat Boone, Johnny Mathis and Connie Francis to Kenneth McKellar, the Big Ben Banjo Band and the Band of the Irish Guards'.

Second in Hunter Davies' list was another pretty Paul tune, 'Michelle' and it seems that with these highly melodic, reflective lyrics, George Martin's influence just grew and grew. The best of them was 'Eleanor Rigby', with its almost Brechtian images of unattended weddings and pauper funerals, its characters isolated from each other in a world where none of them belonged. Paul has said that the influence for the lyric, with its stark, uncompromising hopelessness, came from John, but the impact of the bitterness was made less unbearable by the string quartet accompaniment grafted on by George Martin, drawing upon all his three years at Guildhall School of Music to produce something as far from basic Beatles as 'Daphnis and Chloe' is from 'The Rite of Spring'.

On 'Rigby', however, the schmaltz was not too obtrusive to blunt the song's impact. The bitter lyric bites through the strings like a child asking awkward questions of the pregnant bride at a white wedding, but the questions cut at the heart of the society of lonely people, alienated from each other by the rustle of paper money and the death rattle of work mechanized into meaninglessness. The song is compassionate, and if it doesn't point any tidy little socialist realist solutions like a mid-Victorian morality, it sure enough asks the right questions. As Bob Dylan had already said the three years before, pointing to the new role of these social commentators compared with the serv-it-up-on-a-plate agitprop of the afternoon tea Marxist preachers, '*I can't think for you. You've got to decide.*'

The story was completed by what Lennon was writing at the time, which had the personal viciousness that was beginning to characterize many working class rock lyrics, the sado-sexual myth of revenge. The opening lines of 'Norwegian Wood' should be studied by every feminist who's failed to suss that men need liberating, too, from the same sterile sexual cliches which oppress most women:

> *'I once had a girl,*
> *Or should I say*
> *She once had me?'*

When he burns down the wood-panelled home of the rich bitch who has kicked him out of bed before he's had a chance to touch her, to go sleep in the bath, he echoes Pirate Jenny's exultant *'hop-la!'* as the heads of the bourgeoisie roll in 'Die Dreigroschenoper', and unconsciously uses the same pyromaniacal imagery that Jagger had employed a few years earlier, then, too, addressed to a rich groupie slumming on the rock scene:

> *'Don't play with me*
> *Or you play with fire.'*

This was long before Jim Morrison had turned erotic politics into a mannered pose as void of real sexual content as a stripper scratching inside her G-string.

Next in line of progression from 'Yesterday' via 'Michelle' and 'Eleanor Rigby' was 'She's Leaving Home' on Pepper, which really blew the whole gig. The first time I heard it I convinced myself they had to be taking the piss. A fact. Indeed, even today I still find it hard to believe that even in his slushiest, most sentimental moment, this most sentimental Beatle could get himself so maudlin. But search the lyrics as you will, and there is no secret spine holding the whole jellyfish thing up to ridicule, there are no thorns in the syrup to stick in your throat as you swallow the mellifluous stuff down.

Martin's strings really get out of hand here, oozing great slurps of sound like a Hollywood hack's violin concerto. Of its kind, it's brilliant, the cleverest piece of romantic writing in modern pop, changing from the syrupy backings behind the voices to staccato urgency between the lines, and if there were any hint of real social criticism in the lyric, the arrangement would be a clever counterpoint, like the

Kurt Weill schmaltz that is often employed behind Brecht's bitterest and hardest to swallow didacticism.

This the lyric doesn't do, and while on 'Rigby' the recital of the facts suffices, here he is writing not merely about the break-up of the asexual middle class family left sleeping smugly in their beds while the girl creeps away in the early dawn, he has also involved one of the agents of change herself, the girl, and instead of an insight into what is really happening we get a hackneyed parable, a sob-story about the generation gap, which appears to be merely a break-down of communications on both sides.

Even some of the incidental detail, usually a strong point in their songs, is curiously inappropriate. *'Meeting a man from the motor trade'* is hardly what happens to most girl drop-outs, for the Tricky Dick Nixon image of the car salesman ('Would you buy a used chick from this man?') is the reverse side of the life she has just left, the Mack the Knife sharpie petit-bourgeois shark of which the cosy lifestyle she has just split from is but the soft underbelly. Perhaps he is giving her a lift to the Smoke. Or perhaps those who say *'a man from the motor trade'* means a back-street abortionist are right, though I'm unfamiliar with the term in that context.

The soft complaisant *'bye bye'* of the still sleeping parents at the end pushes it right past the credibility gap and every time I hear it I continue to find it hard to believe (or hope?) there isn't another level of meaning in the song that I'm somehow too dense to see.

Says John: 'If we said when we wrote "She's Leaving Home" we were actually thinking of bananas, nobody would believe us.' *I'm* willing to believe him, but I'm still none the wiser.

On the other hand, with 'Lady Madonna', Paul produced some real insights which weren't equalled when he went over rather similar ground in 'Another Day' after he'd gone solo. The words are an unforgettable picture of domestic drudgery and monotony, the female eunuch chained to the draining board and getting up through the night to feed the latest baby. Perhaps this is what happened to the girl in 'She's Leaving Home' after she married the man from the motor trade.

I can imagine Martin wanting to get his sticky fingers on to it with an 'appropriate' arrangement, but instead they worked it all out in the studio, producing a cooking, rocking sound that could have been almost a hark-back to what they were playing when the heroine of the song was a girl. It has the same 'Hey, where did I hear that before' deja-vu feel to it that their earliest songs did, though actually it's far more sophisticated. They could afford to say 'Don't we need a sax section in there?' and wait while taxis go round to pick up the cream of London's players, jazz people like Ronnie Scott who have survived the death of the big bands to package up their music like a dead art (which it is) and who hate the whole rock thing, but who are proud nevertheless to drop everything and take their horns to the studio to play a riff for the Beatles that is so simple, yet ... so effective, so *right* ... exactly when the notes entered the long-haired heads of the four boys whose music they'd either despised or patronized till then.

As Peter Seeger once said of Woody Guthrie, 'It takes genius to be simple. Any damn fool can get complicated.'

It was about here that the conflicts between them began to become uncontrollable. Lennon's increasing concern with the need for social change, and the inadequacy of most orthodox approaches to revolution, produced a song which upset the leftists but which was much more relevant to the issues than, for instance, the rather simplistic sloganizing of 'Power to the People'. He wanted 'Revolution' to be their next single but the other three plumped for Paul's 'Hey Jude', and 'Revolution' was made the B-side.

Although 'Jude' is a remarkable song by any standards, it lacked the immediate relevance of the other song to a time when the two wings of the anti-Vietnam war movement in Britain were becoming polarized between those who campaigned for peace, and marched pacifically behind Tariq Ali to Downing Street to urge it, and those who wanted NLF victory, who joined the Maoists in trying to smash their way into the American Embassy, a gesture as futile as Tariq Ali's but somehow more dangerous because more dramatic, more self-indulgent because more rewarding to our self-esteem. Misappropriating the cigarette slogan, the marchers urged each other to 'Light up an Embassy' and consoled themselves with the thought that the US Marines had orders not to shoot until anyone started to climb the stairs to the first floor. Actually, the police never let them get to the Embassy steps, even.

Meanwhile, Mick Jagger prowled round the outskirts of the crowd trying to figure it out, and went back to his pad round the corner to work on the lyrics of 'Street Fighting Man':

> 'But what can a poor boy do except sing for a Rock 'n' Roll Band
> 'Cause in sleepy London Town there's just no place for Street Fighting Man!'

Though 'Revolution' was a very valid commentary upon the antics of the tiny radical left in Britain, or possibly because its very validity might have forced us to examine our postures more self-critically, it was 'Jude' that we took to our hearts, for it sang of a sort of quiet confidence that we needed to be able to feel. And the da-da-da sing-out second strain somehow expressed this even better than the words, especially since it made nonsense of the fossilizing structures of the music biz and its press, radio and TV programmes, all of which relied upon the market for singles which mustn't be allowed to run for more than three minutes; meanwhile, all of us bought our music on long-play records because we didn't have autochangers to drop stacks of singles down one by one to the turntable.

There was no technical reason why singles had to have that time limitation forced upon them, for the three-minute straightjacket was merely a historical hangover from a bygone era, being the amount of time one could cram into the grooves of the ten-inch 78s which were the accepted standard for popular music until the 1950s. As a matter of fact, the boundaries which the three-minute discipline forced upon the earliest rock is partly what made them classics, distillations of the form, cramming in as much impact and music as later, lesser performers were to spread so thinly over up to nearly 30 minutes of an LP side. A soloist like Presley's Scotty Moore had to make his point and get back to the vocal in eights bars, at the most, while Clapton and Bloomfield and other more self-conscious artists of rock could take several choruses, often with a minor doldrums round about the middle of the solo while they thought out what to do next.

When Woody recorded his 'Grapes of Wrath' ballad, 'Tom Joad' for Victor, they had to stop him and the recording machine halfway through and put on a second disc so he could finish the story.

Jazzmen had fretted over the constraints of the three-minute formula for years (later, pop musicians were to take over many of the jazzmen's attitudes to the business, bad as well as good) which bore little relation to the long free-wheeling solos they could blow after hours in Mintons. But to listen to the several unissued masters of a single number by Charlie Parker is to realize how brilliantly could such a genius structure what he had to say within one or two choruses, how carefully the total edifice was worked out in advance and how little was left to chance inspiration. Often the tight format gave his solos a consciseness he lacked on the longer, more self-indulgent jam sessions issued by Norman Granz as 'Jazz at the Philharmonic'.

Nevertheless, the substitution of the 45 rpm vinylite disc for the 78 shellac made the three-minute limitation a pointless anachronism: it was possible to get up to eight minutes on the little seven-inch discs without appreciable loss in fidelity.

'Hey Jude' showed how it could be done commercially. When the record was first issued in Britain, the only disc jockey who played it in its entirety was John Peel. It was on his underground show that I heard it first and I remember thinking it sounded quite nice, nothing special. I like the da-da-da bit: a happy way to finish the record.

Hey, they're doing another chorus of the singalong, what a gas! Now they're doing it again! This is getting like Count Basie's 'April in Paris' – one *more* time! They've got to be kidding. Oh, too much!

On all the other shows they faded it quickly at the end of the first chorus – for about a week. Then when it hit the top of the charts so explosively, the radio establishment caved in and had to play the damn thing the whole way through. It was a mighty victory, from which bubble-gum radio has not yet fully recovered.

Despite all this, the Revolution: Hey Jude controversy – which we didn't hear about until after the group split up – was the beginning of a divergence that got wider and wider. While Paul tended to say 'That's the way life is', John was protesting louder and louder 'That's not the way life ought to be'. 'Let It Be' was the last song in which they could find some common ground, and that only because it was a lyric that could have so many different things read into it.

For instance, many thought it had a quasi-religious flavour to it, because of the line *'mother Mary comes to me'* and black singers have done it as quite an effective gospel number. The *Rolling Stone* critic said that 'Martin Luther and John Calvin may be represented in the 'amen' chord changes, but the lyrics are strictly Catholic. In a time of torment and darkness the Virgin Mary returns to the Earth with her simple message of deliverance. *"There will be an answer. Let it be, let it be."* ' The only trouble is that here Paul is not referring to the Holy Virgin but to his own beloved mother, who died of cancer when he was 14, whose memory was still a help to him in times of trouble.

Similarly, while for Paul *'Let it be'* was a statement of acceptance, akin to Dylan Thomas's 'Isn't life a terrible thing thank God', to John it was a valediction: What's done is done, what's past is past, so don't let's try to keep it alive in a world so different from the world of Mersey-mania, let it stand, let it end, let it be. Now let's move on to something different.

The next time John offered them a song they didn't quite dig, 'Cold Turkey', he thought 'Bugger you, I'll put it out myself'. Which he did, though when at approximately the same time in 1970 he wanted to do 'You Know My Name (Look Up the Number)' as a solo single, he agreed to let it be the B-side of 'Let It Be' because when originally recorded, the Beatles had still been a functioning entity.

It was paradoxical that while John had been the one all along most willing to finish up the Beatles partnership once Brian Epstein died, it was Paul who took the action to dissolve it legally when it was clear even to him eventually that Apple had failed to produce the corporative substitute for Epstein they had hoped it would be.

In the film 'Let It Be', Paul had seemed to be assuming Epstein's mantle: '... we've been very negative since Mr Epstein passed away.... It's like when you're growing up and then your daddy goes away at a certain point and then you stand on your own feet. Daddy has gone away now, you know, and we are on our own little holiday camp. You know, I think we either go home or we do it. It's discipline we need. It's like everything you do, you never had discipline. Mr Epstein, he said, sort of "Get suits on" and we did. And so we were always fighting that discipline a bit. But now it's silly to fight that discipline if it's our own. It's self-imposed these days, so we do as little as possible. But I think we need a bit more if we are going to get on with it.'

The con. Paul's attempt to keep it going illuminates and shines right through the film's pretences like a million megapower searchlight, for 'Let It Be' is a very artificial film, a rather untrue film, the incredible tensions building up between the four boys become men are skated over or only very briefly referred to. There is even a bit of synthetic Alun Owen-type dialogue, reading like a dramatization of 'John Lennon in His Own Write':

John: Bognor Regis is a tartan that covers Yorkshire. Rutland is the smallest county. Scarborough is a college scarf.

And still the boom wasn't over, the Queen of Sheba wore falsies.

Ringo: I didn't know that.

John: Didn't you know that? You weren't there at the time. Cleopatra was a carpet manufacturer.

Ringo: I didn't know that.

John: John Lennon.

Ringo: A patriot.

John: I didn't know that.

Paradoxically, though Paul tried hardest to keep the Beatles going after the death of Epstein, and he was Epstein's ally in the issue of the suits, that isn't the way John remembers it at all. When Apple began to fall apart it was John who brought in Allen Klein, the sharp trans-atlantic operator, to put things right, rather like an Old Bolshevik of the 1920s hiring ex-Tsarist secret police to run the OGPU when the revolution ran into choppy water: the end justifies the means.

'Three of us chose Epstein,' John recalled. 'Paul was the same with Brian in the beginning, if you must know. He used to sulk and God knows what. Wouldn't turn up for the dates or bookings. It's always been the same only now it's bigger because we're all bigger.'

But Apple was basically Paul's idea, which was ironic

because it was the order from the other three as Apple
directors, instructing Paul not to issue his 'McCartney'
solo album at a time that might conflict with 'Let It Be',
that finally pissed Paul off so much that he took the whole
issue to Court to get sorted.

Apple was another relic of that flower power summer
when everyone was talking about setting up alternative
systems, when it seemed that any of the straight state's
evils would disappear if you just blew enough pot smoke
in their faces. Originally, it was a sort of collective and
the Beatle earnings were to be the core of a great free
community of hip artists and pop technicians. That was
why the controlling company was called Apple Corps Ltd
(corps=core, get it?). They advertised in all the underground papers for talent. James Taylor came over to record
but hated the result, even though it contained some of his
best songs, like 'Going to Carolina in My Mind'. Taylor
went back home for more mental treatment.

The first tangible thing they did, even before opening
the Savile Row offices in the heart of the West End's
prestigious custom tailoring district (£150 for a suit, six
weeks to wait, and they won't even deign to notice you if
your shoes are dirty or your hair is long) was to open a
boutique in Baker Street mostly to sell clothes designed by
Simon and Marijka, known collectively as The Fool. Some
of them were used in 'Magical Mystery Tour'. The Fool
were into graphics, too, and they had hassles with the
Borough Council over the psychedelic astrological graffiti
they painted over one entire wall of the building (eventually
they agreed to over-paint it plain white). The Fool designed
the sleeve for the Incredible String Band's second album
and already it looks dated, not in that nostalgic 'remember
when' feeling you get from early Peter Max and Family
Dog posters: just that time has stripped the glamour and
phoney significance off, leaving the facile superficial glossy
imagery, the faces like advertising agency visual roughs

before the character is drawn in, staring us brazenly in the eyes and saying exactly nothing, nothing at all.

Bringing The Fool clothes to London was a pretty dumb idea, because the same sort of multi-layered psychedelic gypsy look was already being done much better on Kings Road, in shops like Granny Takes a Trip (where if you were hip enough to know what the name meant you could also get acid: it was still legal then). And anyway, the London kids were able to create just as pretty things for themselves from cast-offs bought in the Oxfam shops and the antique supermarkets. Lovely stuff that was second-hand was somehow more chic, because it carried along auras of the past; these were clothes with histories to them. The girl who let you see her tits through the black chiffon petticoat she wore as a dress, without any bra, knew that the garment's original owner would have been shocked at her brazenness: that was part of the fun.

The Apple boutique was a small failure, but the impulsiveness of the whole damn thing, the refusal to consult any of the young fashion professionals in a city whose Carnaby Street had rocked Seventh Avenue and the rue du Fabourg St Honore to their very foundations, the crazy notion that there was any point in importing fashion designers from Amsterdam (a nice enough city, with fairly cool police and the best hip radicals in the world, but no fashion centre, for God's sake), when London was full of them, was typical of the utopian unreality of almost everything they did then. And the fact that it was in clothes, one of the most peripheral aspects of revolutionary youth culture, and the most susceptible to rip-offs by balding enterpreneurs, that they started, was kind of significant of what was to come.

Anyway, one day they realized the boutique was losing money so they decided to close it up, right then, and to avoid all that tedious business of close out sales they announced that anyone who called in could take anything they wanted for free. Well, at least their talent for getting press inches hadn't deserted them.

Meanwhile, much bigger losses were mounting up to worry them. In its first year, Apple was said to have lost a million dollars. The Beatles were coming to realize that an alternative community had to be a closed system, that if it tried to have truck with the big corporations, to compete with people like EMI on their terms, they would always lose, unless they thought like businessmen. John Lennon brought in Allen Klein to sort things out.

He negotiated them a better American records deal, upping their royalty from 40 to 56 cents a record sold, to rise ultimately to 72 cents. To cover the increase, Capitol Records increased their prices and some of the American kids started a Beatles boycott. According to an affidavit presented to the Court by Klein in early 1971, their earnings rose as soon as he began to manage them. They had been just under £400 thousand in the year 1968-9 and in the first nine months of Klein's management they topped half a million: in 1970 this escalated to nearly £4¼ million (to be fair, these years also showed a rising graph of individual artistic activity, one of the reasons for the remarkable boost to profits shown in Klein's evidence).

'Let It Be' – record and film – was the last vestiges of what the Beatles and Apple had been and might be. The original idea had been to get back to the roots of Beatlemania, to record a live show and film it at the same time as a TV spectacular. The Roundhouse, London's nearest equivalent to Bill Graham's now-closed Fillmores in USA, was booked for the show, then cancelled, then rebooked, cancelled again because, it was said, the weather was so cold (it was January). After the months of work and overdubbing and tape snipping that had gone into 'Pepper' this was to have been the Beatles as they really were, warts and all, the world's most famous rock and roll band, but the plan didn't seem to be working very well.

OK, the live gig was blown, but they could still do it

F

live in the studio, couldn't they, with the minimum of electronic trickery, showing where they were really at? So they did, and they brought in Michael Lindsay-Hogg, whose work on a couple of their promotional films they'd liked, and filming started on January 2, 1969, in Twickenham Studios where Ringo was filming 'The Magic Christian' with Peter Sellers and didn't want to be too far away from the set.

In addition to the original idea about a TV special, they decided also to make a documentary about making the TV special about the album. Eventually the special was never made, though it is an unseen character throughout the documentary. The Beatles were being Pirandellian again, as they often did when things started to get difficult (this was actually four months before Klein started tidying it up).

Right in the middle of everything, one of the Beatles quit, said he was splitting the group, they could finish the album without him, the movie without him, that's it, finish. Who? Not John; not Paul. It was George Harrison who brought things to a head.

Lindsay-Hogg had this grandiose idea for a grand finale, with the Beatles going really *right* back to their roots, back past Liverpool, back to Africa, with the whole goddam continent singing along with the da-da-da of 'Hey Jude'. Da da da *da*-da-da dah – that was Tunisia. *Da-da*-da dah – Nigeria. Da *dah* – Biafra. The plane was hired, ready to take off. And George quit.

This much later, it's easy to see why he cracked first. He was the best musician out of the four, or anyway certainly the most *musicianly,* and as the group began to break up (which it was already beginning to do, artistically, at the time of their white double album) the other three became merely backing musicians to whoever was in the spotlight at the time – and that meant for three-quarters of the time.

As John told Jann Wenner of *Rolling Stone* magazine

much later: 'Every track is an individual track – there isn't any Beatle music on it. . . . It was John and the band, Paul and the band, George and the band, like that. . . . What I did was sort of say "Fuck the band, I'll make John – I'll do it with Yoko" or whatever.'

In the film, George says testily to Paul: 'All right, I'll play whatever you want me to play, or I won't play at all if you don't want me to play.' Paul always was a bit of a musical clever Dick, showing Ringo exactly the licks he wanted on the drums.

Also, George is the most religious member of the group, with whom most of the mystical memories of the Maharishi business have remained. He is still liable to start chanting mantras to himself to calm himself down when he can't cope. He was the most likely to have recognized the Lindsay-Hogg idea for the inflated moviemaker's ego trip it was, the sort of incredibly expensive non-concepts people seem to get when they're working with the Beatles.

Nevertheless, they had their 'honest' album, didn't they, yer actual Beatles, recorded on location at Twickenham Studios, far away from the familiarity of Abbey Road, and in the new Apple Studios, where George Martin had to come in at the last moment and get the electronics working right. The trouble was, none of them liked it. Well, perhaps Paul did, because he certainly didn't like what Phil Spector did to it.

In many ways, Spector is one of the greatest musicians of this electronic age, playing the archetypal musical instrument of the age: the recording studio. There are a few other practitioners, Brian Wilson of the Beach Boys, George Martin himself, and of course there are studios (and the local session musicians) which seem to have a life of their own, imparting their own particular flavour to the music in rather a similar way to one of the great producers like Spector. But he is the greatest, the only record man to deserve being called an *auteur,* along with the great film producers beloved of *Les Cahiers du Cinema.*

There is, however, an inhumanity running through his work, in which the musicians and singers are almost incidentals. Effect is piled upon effect, the whole thing is run through so many limiters, with so many multitrack overdubs, that what we hear is ennervating, it is so soulless.

He took Ike and Tina Turner and their comparatively little-known black road show and gave them a hit with 'River Deep Mountain High' but though the drums thud much thuddier than any recorded drums you ever heard before, though Ike's bass guitar figure running between the verses hits you deep in the gut with its subsonics, though the Ikettes shrieking the chorus sound like a million Valkyries, it is not as exciting as Ike and Tina Turner can be. I am not comparing it with them in the flesh. It is not merely that this ugly little black girl is the sexiest, raunchiest, most vulgar piece of ass that ever wiggled in front of a microphone, not excluding the late Janis Joplin (these days Tina wears tights; she was even sexier in the days when the guys at front of stage could gaze up her skirt to see the suspenders and the bare thigh between stocking top and knicker, looking like she not only didn't care about them looking but actually getting turned on by it). It would be difficult to catch all of that on record.

But I have heard less brilliantly produced recordings of the Turners which have revealed more of the sweaty soul of their craft. 'River Deep Mountain High' packages it all up behind an unrelenting wall of electronic sound, and while the result succeeds in penetrating the tinny tiny speakers of most AM transistors radios, the effect is not at all stimulating in a gut way. You admire it, you say wow, you are impressed, then you switch to the Stones' 'Brown Sugar' or the Beatles' 'Get Back' for music to move your body to. Heard stereo, the entire album Spector produced of Ike and Tina is, ultimately, too overpowering to take in one go. Perhaps that is why it bombed in USA.

He does good singles, though, and the Plastic Ono things he's done for John really work as singles, though obscuring some of the most vital words of 'Instant Karma' with flutter echo tends to blunt the message.

What he did with the Beatles' last album, however, was something rather different. For a start, none of the original musical concepts involved him, not at all. He was merely handed all the recording tapes, the takes and the mistakes and the out-takes, and asked in a sort of desperation to do something with them. The change in titles is indicative of the way the Beatles felt about it when he'd finished.

'Get Back', which had started as the chorus of a song about immigrants and Powellite racism, was also to have been the name of the album. It was an injunction to get back to the roots. 'Let It Be' as we have seen, came to be an injunction to leave well alone. After what Phil Spector had done to the album, it seemed like a good idea.

Possibly Paul's marriage was the real key to the break-up. Certainly the Apple Scruffs, the girls who hang round Savile Row waiting for a glance or even a word from a real live Beatle, felt that it was the beginning of the end in a way that the other's marriages, and John's divorce and marriage to Yoko, never had been. They rushed round to Paul's place in St John's Wood to weep and ask him if it was true, but Paul like a berk got hold of the wrong end of the stick, thinking they were jealous of Linda, but it was more that they'd accepted Jane Asher as his girl friend for such a long time that this strange American chick had to be bad news for the rest of Beatledom, if not for Paul.

Linda's family were show biz lawyers, and Paul tried to row them in to take Klein's place, but no success. So when he issued his first album it contained a four-page self interview, explaining the break up as if it was something that had only just happened.

John summed up the big announcement wryly: 'The cartoon is this: four guys on a stage with a spotlight on them. Second picture: three guys on stage breezing out of the spotlight. Third picture: one guy standing there, shouting 'I'm leaving'. We were all out of it.'

It had taken a long time, nearly three years after Epstein's death, but the con was finally over. The today image was definitely yesterday. And 'Yesterday' was scrambled eggs, as it always had been.

VI

Crazy John

"Who do you think you are?
A Superstar? Well, right you are!"
                              –Instant Karma

TOM PAXTON has this song about John Lennon which
warns him of the dangers of acting crazy, walking on the
water and stuff, like that other visionary they crucified.

'*When the people get lost,*' goes the song,
'*They start building a cross.*'

Paxton has a keener critical brain than the slushier of his
romantic lovesongs might lead you to suspect, and anyway
if you listen to them carefully they're not really that slushy
really. It's just that we find it so much less embarrassing
to say 'fuck' than 'love' these days.

Nevertheless, here he's wrong, for Lennon's antics aren't
the holy foolishness of a crucifixion candidate. Lennon
does many of the crazy things he does to *prevent* people
from taking him so seriously that they nail him up, just
to be safe. It's like the advice on survival techniques Asinius
Pollio gives to poor shambling, stammering, slobbering
Claudius in the Robert Graves novel: '... exaggerate your
limp, stammer deliberately, sham sickness frequently, let

your wits wander, jerk your head, and twitch your hands on all public and semi-public occasions. If you could see as much as I can see you would know that this was your only hope of safety and eventual glory.' Lennon has had enough glory to last him a lifetime, but safety, in an era of disintegrating states where the in-fighting is even more vicious than in the break-up of the Roman Republic – *that* he needs.

Take the notorious case of his MBE and the message he sent when he returned it to the Queen, saying he was making a gesture of protest against the wars in Vietnam and Biafra, and against 'Cold Turkey' slipping down the charts. The note of bathos was deliberate. At one level, the reference to 'Cold Turkey' was an apologetic embarrassment at the great rage which had built up inside him in the face of human cruelty, a rage so great that he just couldn't stand it any more, the sort of deliberate self-conscious defusing of an emotional situation that is common among English provincials, for whom such heights and depths are, literally, uncool.

At another level, Lennon was saying something important to himself artistically, for to him 'Cold Turkey', a song he'd offered to the Beatles but they'd turned it down so he'd gone it alone, was just as important as the wars. It was smaller in absolute terms, of course, but because it was closer to him it seemed to loom just as large in perspective. As a matter of fact, 'Cold Turkey' wasn't slipping when he said that, not at all, and the following week it rose a place in the British charts. There'd been an element of Merseyside canniness in ensuring that all the reports of him returning the medal would mention his latest record, and undoubtedly it helped.

It was also a commentary upon the pomposity of those holders who'd returned *their* medals in protest against Harold Wilson giving the MBE to the Beatles (for services to British exports) in June 1965, which was funny because John had been against accepting the honour in the first place. When the royal letter arrived, he pretended not to realize how important it was, just filing it 'with the other fanmail' to be dealt with when he had the time. Eventually they got together and decided to accept it, but John only agreed after he realized that accepting it would upset more people than refusing it would do. Theoretically, you never get a chance to actually refuse any royal honour, because the way you are asked in the first place is so circuitous, so non-commital, asking what your hypothetical attitude might perhaps be if they were to consider thinking of possibly offering you the medal, that you can never claim to have had anything so definite as an offer to have been able to actually say No. Dashed clever, these British royals. They've been in the survival business for a long time.

So they accepted the bloody things and John gave his to his Aunt Mimi to put on top of the telly. They did their best to devalue the presentation, having a quick drag of a joint in the Buckingham Palace loo so they were stoned when they met the Queen but that didn't help much, seeing as how nobody knew about it but them. To John it had always been the ultimate sell-out, the least accept-able part of the great Beatles con.

Later, he was to say that the only thing that excused his accepting it had been the fact that it allowed him to make the returning gesture four years later.

Then there was the survival tactic: 'If we played it straight like Gandhi and Martin Luther King,' he said, 'we wouldn't be here. The thing is people don't like saints. And we're not going to be saints, crucified or otherwise. So we keep throwing in a bit of shit.

'On the one hand, "Cold Turkey" has got nothing to do with it. On the other, "Cold Turkey" is as much about dying in Biafra or Vietnam as it is about withdrawal from drugs.'

But it *was* about withdrawal from drugs, the hardest ones like heroin, and the term cold turkey is such common parlance for the agonies of withdrawal, the pain, the shivering fevers, the gnawing, insatiable hungers from basic changes in the body's metabolism created by the drug so that you need it just to stay normal, with nothing like a high involved, that it's surprising the BBC didn't ban it right away. It was hardly an advertisement for hard drugs, but that hasn't stopped other drug songs like 'The Pusher' from getting themselves banned.

This was the other thing that was important about 'Cold Turkey', for John and Yoko's brief flirtation with hard drugs which culminated with the song was the end of that whole drug phase in his development. The acid dream, he was later to admit, was finally over.

There was a similar mix of complex motivations in exposing himself and Yoko's nakednesses on the cover of their first joint album, 'Two Virgins'. Here was this guy, one of the four most famous and popular pop musicians in the history of the world, who could have any chick he wanted just for the asking and *had,* during those dionysian odysseys, the Beatles tours, and stripped off he don't look so hot, no better hung than most of us, any road. And that Japanese chick: in this age of silicone inflated tits photographed upside down so they don't sag, or held up with Scotch tape and nylon thread so they don't sag like my old lady's do, she has big, drooping udder-shaped breasts that look pretty functional alright, but here's this guy could have any of those Playboy centrefold girls and this is what he chooses? She's not even white. And look, fellers, they both got *hair* down there like you and me (later, Hugh M. Hefner told his art department to moderate their wielding of the airbrush just a fraction, though earlier he'd given a negative reply to a correspondent who'd asked wouldn't it be more realistic to leave the pubic hair un-touched out. Hefner had said he couldn't see why only ugly and unpleasant things were considered realistic, begging the question).

Stripped there like that, not in any conventionally pretty or even erotic pose, just staring slightly startled at the camera as if it had poked its snout through their bathroom window, they were remarkably *vulnerable*, like Adam and Eve just before the Fall, as if they'd bunked out over the wall of Paradise to have a look at the wicked world outside before they scrumped apples and discovered shame and made themselves figleaves. Two virgins, the title and the picture said it all.

Lennon's exposures were not at all like the depersonalized stripping off that has become obligatory of any cinema or theatre with pretences towards avant garde; in contrast with the compulsive sexual totalitarianism of these pieces, there was a strange, idyllic innocence about the way he displayed his body, even though that didn't stop the display from upsetting the philistines, bringing the police round to the art gallery which showed his erotic lithographs (case dismissed).

He has always been quite a good artist, in a James Thurber lavatory graffiti sort of way. After all, he'd been good enough to go to art college until the call came to go to Hamburg, Where It All Began, even if he didn't win any sixty quid prizes like Stu Sutcliffe. Possibly because of Yoko, there was a new spare feel about the lithographs, sort of zen, that impression you get from Oriental art of a guy with a brush loaded with black ink (the bottle's empty) so he must make every single stroke count before the ink runs out.

The one of John going down between Yoko's legs made that forbidden pastime look as innocent and supplicatory as it actually is, strangely touching and not at all obscene. The gallery owner said they were 'pornographic but not obscene' and if looking so sweet you want to get right down and lick the next girl you meet as quickly as possible is pornography, I suppose he was right, because they made me feel thataway quite definitely.

It reminded me of that line from 'At the Denis' in 'John Lennon in His Own Write' which is actually supposed to be about a woman's mouth, but perhaps because of the mouse-pussy connotation, always makes me think of cunt:

'*Sir:* Sly down in that legchair Madam and open your gorble wide – your mouse is all but toothless.' No vagina dentata nonsense here!

Almost inevitably, this freaky trend in his public behaviour was ascribed to Yoko, but he'd always been something of a tearaway, learning dirty jokes (from a *girl*) before all his mates, going round pulling girl's knickers down at school, that sort of thing. Yoko brought innocence to it.

It was the same sort of innocence that had caused the 'Film No 1' she made with her former husband, Tony Cox, of 365 arses or thereabouts to be such a commercial failure. It sounded salacious, but it just wasn't. It wasn't even vaguely erotic.

They advertised in *The Stage* for volunteers for an *avante garde* movie and then asked them to walk for a few seconds on a sort of continuous belt, backs to the camera, stripped to the buff. The belt revolved as they walked, keeping them a constant distance from camera. The shot was in big close-up, so the actual image on screen was of a gently palpitating cross, the vertical member made up of the shadow between the buttocks, the horizontal line the shadows under the two cheeks of each arse. The result was peaceful, innocent, hypnotic, some kind of moving mandala, as one image flashed on to the screen after the other.

They blew it, however, by one aspect of the movie which probably sounded like a rather cute idea at the time; which is what it was, a cute idea. The film had a sound-track: made up of the tape-recorded spontaneous replies of those who answered the ads when they were told what was required of them. It was hilarious, to be honest. 'It's a bit *smutty*,' said one woman with Bedfordshire hauteur. 'I'm a professional,' said a fruity old actor's voice, 'and I really believe that even in a role like this, acting ability is still valuable.' He obviously needed the gig.

The trouble was that this wasn't the soundtrack for that movie, even if it made the film more saleable. It turned a work that bore serious comparison with Warhol's Empire State and 'Sleep' movies into something much more smart aleck, much less. I like to think that the soundtrack was Cox's idea, but anyway it was a real cop-out.

Her next movie was focussed on John's prick, which is particularly interesting to me because 'Film No 1' had inspired in me my first, and so far unfulfilled screen idea, with the working title 'Erections'. I'd planned to film a series of slowly stiffening cocks, building up a compulsive rhythm as they rose, one after another, great throbbing cyclops, a hymn of love to maleness and the surge of spring, Dylan Thomas's 'force that through the green fuse drives the flower'. As Albert Ellis says, 'Up yours' ought to be a compliment.

The idea was conceptual, like many of the things in Yoko's 'grapefruit' book of poems. Once you've thought of it, you don't really need to do it. The great hang-up with conceptual art – or its greatest strength, if you prefer – is the fact that the application of the concept is actually far less effective than the basic idea in your head. That guy who parcels up bits of landscape in polythene, the idea of hundreds of miles of coatline wrapped up that way is itself so mind-blowing, that actually to see it, piece by piece rather than in its totality, is something of an anti-climax. The film of the gig on TV was most interesting at the beginning and the end, during the incredible task of tying the vast sheets of polythene down over the cliffs, and again later when nature herself took a hand, and sent a storm to rip the plastic away from round her holy loins. But that was a different trip, as unconnected with the original concept as the soundtrack of 'Film No 1'. I heard that he went back and tied it all down again, in faithfulness to his original concept, but I think that nature's intervention created a greater concept, though the single shot from the air in the middle of the movie of the plasticized cliffs for one single serene moment did have a remarkable impact, a gloriously ultimate absurdity, like Claes Oldenberg's fag-ends the size of the Empire State Building and coke bottles by the side of the Thames, dwarfing Big Ben.

It was actually at an Oldenberg show in London that John and Yoko first met, properly that is. He'd gone to a preview of her show at John Dunbar's art gallery and she'd handed him a card saying 'Breathe' on it, and he'd panted in her face, tongue out like a dog in heat. But that hadn't been a proper meeting, just one of those cocktail party encouters that have to take the place of communication in the higher echelons of good ole swingin' London. Then at the Oldenberg opening they saw each other, really flashed on each other across a crowded room like in the song, and a little while later she called on him as so many others did during the fruiting of the Apple period, seeking backing for one of her projects. She gave him a copy of 'Grapefruit' and he got involved in some of the things she was doing.

By the time he and his wife Cynthia were going to India with the Maharishi they had got to the just good friends bit. Possibly he was more aware of the stage they'd reached than he now admits, because he wanted to take Yoko to India with him and Cyn but at the last minute he decided it wasn't cool and chickened out. He must have realized something was happening.

Cynthia was someone important to him from way back, possibly part of the part of him that had agreed to Brian Epstein's suits and accepting the MBE, the fearful frightened snobbishness of the Liverpool proletarian about the land of milk and honey across the Mersey from which she came. In those art school days they'd studied lettering together but though they went into the same classrooms they moved in different circles, she the refined middle class girl and he the Ted tearaway, living his life even then with an intensity that was somehow terrifying. Such a man will sometimes cleave to someone quite alien, less intense, to help quell the terror of self he feels within him. I did it myself once.

It had been an attraction of opposites, and it always seemed like a pot on the boil, always about to brim over. Like many such relationships, the tension produced an internal dynamic which could keep it going, to all intents and appearances perfectly, until it exploded.

She tended to keep him on an even show-biz keel, especially after Brian died, helping him be the walrus, getting him to go to new clubs he wouldn't normally be seen dead in, that sort of thing. He began to retreat inside himself as he started to shrug out of the walrus costume, seeking the self-alienation which is light years away from meditation, seeing his hands move at the ends of his arms as if belonging to some Beatle robot, the retreat from reality.

He'd been messing about with electronic sounds in the upstairs studio at his £60,000 home in Weybridge for a long time before he locked horns with Yoko's particular brand of intense, New York haiku avant garde simplicity, and when one night she rang him he invited her down to have a listen. After she'd heard them they both started work immediately on the tapes that became 'Two Virgins'. It was midnight. They finished at dawn.

Then they made love. Cyn was away at the time.

Their love came as a shock to everyone, not so much because of breaking up John and Cyn but because it looked as if Yoko might really upset the whole goddam gravy train. They'd never been much for the marital fidelity bit. John himself has described the Beatles on tour as like something out of 'Fellini Satyricon' which is what makes the clean-cut kid image they had then such a joke. 'Norwegian Wood' was about an affair John was having at the time, though the story was muddied up to protect the feelings of the innocent, namely Cyn. Everyone was in on the con, the four Beatles themselves, the road managers, the MPs and VIPs, and the journalists. Especially the journalists. There were so many groupies going spare round the Beatles you just had to pull one – at least one. It was a floating orgy.

With Cyn, John had always insisted on being a Beatle first and foremost, always popping round to Ringo's, vanishing inside himself very quickly if only she was around. Yoko was different: John put her first, before anything, and the rest saw it and resented it. Though later they graciously decided to admit her into the clan it was too late. John had realized he didn't need them any more.

Something else he learnt to do without was religion, although he became more and more truly religious. As recently as the Hunter Davies book he'd declared that his biggest interest was Nirvana, that he might just give up all this millionaire shit and become poor again, a Buddha.

The Maharishi bit had already been a big disillusionment, the giggly old man chasing birds when he wasn't sellling instant karma, refusing to even try to understand what all the fuss was about when they told him Brian was dead, that day in Bangor, the media of the world looking on to see how they'd react to the news, they turning to him for some kind of comfort and getting a few Orientally-tinged phrases straight out of Dale Carnegie. 'Sexy Sadie' on the double white album is about him, though once again the message was obscured to protect the guilty. That was a game John was still playing.

When he announced he was leaving the Beatles the rest of them persuaded John to keep it to himself so he did, only to see Paul make his own big announcement at exactly the right time to help sell his first solo album. When John describes Paul as the best PR man in the world he's not being snide, because he knows he once might have merited the title himself, and anyway he admires the boy's expertise in a sort of detached, amused way. It's something he can say now he's on a different trip.

In 'Glass Onion' he'd formally handed over the whole

scene to Paul, saying 'The walrus is Paul'. In 'I am the Walrus' the beast was undoubtedly John, despite the Pirandellian overtones, using the image of Lewis Carroll's 'Walrus and the Carpenter', the archetypal hot rod trouble-shooting wizz kid *entrepreneur* who eats up all the teeny-bopper oysters and gently dabs the juice off his chin with a freshly laundered linen napkin. Allen Klein rather than Brian Epstein. For all its idealism, Apple had been the height of all that and it ended, in spirit if not in fact, with Yoko, though the realization had to force itself upon him.

The scenes changed, but he still tried to be the *guntse-macher,* using his international fame and charisma to achieve things denied of lesser mortals.

He began to concern himself with peace. Their first press conference after the wedding in Gibraltar had been the Amsterdam Bed-In when John and Yoko met the press in their room in bed on the seventh floor of the Amsterdam Hilton, just sitting in pyjamas talking about peace. It was Peter Watkins, maker of 'The War Game' movie that the BBC commissioned and then refused to show, who had pointed out to them that the media were still controlled by the same grey arthritic hands. He had urged them as the hottest media properties since Adolf Hitler to do their best to freak the whole scene out. 'All You Need Is Love' was the first result, but John was dissatisfied somehow, perhaps because the imagery was rather closer to 'I Wanna Hold Your Hand' than to the real issues Watkins had raised. The message was still being concealed.

He thought of going to Biafra, but Yoko was having problems with her pregnancy. Then she had a miscarriage. Anyway, it was a problem, because the obvious place to go seemed to be wherever the action was thickest, Biafra, or Vietnam, or Czechoslovakia, or wherever. But that seemed a good way of being martyred, which John had long realized was a very present danger.

Yoko had turned him on to the idea of events, happen-ings around which was dramatized whatever drama there

G

was in a given situation, which were their own justification. As soon as he got the MBE, John had started looking for an event which could be his reason for giving it back. Then he realized that giving it back, *that* was the event. So he did it.

When the press went to the seventh floor room in Amsterdam they were expecting something pretty far out. By that time anything John and Yoko did was an event because they did it, and events had already begun to invent themselves. When Richard Williams of *Melody Maker* received the test pressing of their wedding album on two single-sided LPs instead of the usual single double-sided white label record, he solemnly included reviews of both the blank sides in his review, and after all why not? Hadn't John Cage proved that silence had its own music? The fact that John and Yoko hadn't planned it that way somehow made the whole thing even more believable. Conceptual art again, but this time the concept was ... superhuman, infinite, a divine accident.

Rumours were rife. The most commonly anticipated event was going to be John and Yoko having it away right there, before the eyes and ears of the world (later they did it on record which satisfied the ear freaks).

What happened was even more far out. Nothing (in news media terms) happened at all, which made it a bigger story than ever. Another blank record side. All they did was sit there and rabbit about peace, right? Far fucking out!

Shortly after followed Toronto, the Peace Festival debacle, about which thousands of words have been written and which would require a whole book of its own to sort out exactly what went wrong and whose fault it was, if it matters.

Some of it was the last dregs of the acid-Nirvana trip, because on John's insistence the organisers included for a time members of the California Harbinger Springs cult, who forthwith decided that they would capture the Earth Force surrounding the Beatles and use it in conjunction with superhuman beings from another world to bring long-awaited peace to the planet. John and Yoko were to fly into Mosport Park in a psychic-powered air car which would only cost $500 and never needed any fuel. The overall length of the plane was to be 22 feet, an important factor in Egyptian numerology, and the tailplane was set at an angle with another magical significance.

Two of the Harbinger people went to Denmark to talk about it to the Lennons when they were visiting Tony Cox and Yoko's daughter by him, Kyoko. As an example of their powers one of them tried to cure John of his nicotine habit by hypnotizing him into remembering his previous lives. The whole thing was fairly disastrous and though John decided they were not the people to help him with the festival, and in particular to control the 'bread hang-up' he saw developing in what would necessarily have to be a multi-million dollar project, he continued to believe that they might possibly have something, that there might be some truth in their claim to have been aboard a space-ship, talking to the superhuman aliens, though Yoko was less willing to suspend her unbelief. That was in early January, 1970.

The idea of a peace festival – originally called the Peace Grease (a 'grease' is a promotional party, organized by a record company to 'grease' the palms of the media freaks, get it?) – had come from a group of Canadians who talked to John and Yoko at Apple a month before. It seemed to figure. John and Yoko had already been there for the Rock 'n' Roll Revival organized by John Brower, and though, much later, the wise-after-the-event folk pointed to everything that went wrong *then,* he seemed the logical guy to get it together. And Canada seemed nice. Canada was giving asylum to a lot of US draftees on the run and, unlike Sweden or Britain, was making no effort to send them home.

'The Immigration Department there has been a lot nicer to us than other countries,' said John. The US was then still refusing to give a visa to him because of a dope bust.

'Canada's attitudes with regard to Vietnam, China and NATO are very sensible. Everything points to Canada as being one of the key countries in the new race for survival. We've had the arms race and the space race and the cold war – the time has come for the peace race.'

Once the thing started, John didn't hang about. Twelve days after that meeting, he flew into Toronto with Yoko for meetings with Marshall McLuhan, the electronic maharishi, and with the Canadian Prime Minister. Nobody said anything publicly right then about superhuman beings from another planet, though John expressed the hope that the other Beatles would come to Toronto with him to jam the following July. The fact that he'd announced to Allen Klein on the plane over that he was determined to split from the group did not diminish his confidence that they'd come, it seemed.

Already a gap was opening, between John Brower and the Canadians planning the festival on the one hand and the Lennons on the other, though neither was aware of it that early. And it wasn't so much anything to do with psychic-powered aircraft as with the role of John and the Beatles themselves, his dawning realization that any super-star was on an ego-trip that could only destroy anything he tried to accomplish, however idealistically motivated.

In their Toronto press conference, John had made his position clear, which was to shun the leadership syndrome. 'I believe that leaders and father figures are the mistake of all the generations before us. And that all of us rely on Nixon or Jesus or whoever we rely on; it's lack of responsibility that you expect somebody else to do it. He must help me or we kill him or we vote him out. . . .

'I won't be a leader. Everybody is a leader. People thought the Beatles were leaders, but they weren't, and now people are finding that out.'

For their part, they were so confident of the pulling

power of the Beatles, the festival organizers didn't really work too hard on signing up supporting acts, though they talked airily of the Stones and Dylan and the Grateful Dead coming along too. They talked rather less about the specifics they'd need to cope with the two million people they hoped to attract from all over North America and the world: specifics like the 10,000 toilets that would be needed, though Brower planned to sell the contents of the bogs to fertilizer firms to help swell the coffers of Karma Productions, 50 per cent of which would go to the Peace Foundation the Lennons were planning to set up, though at that stage the money wasn't the main point. The main point was the event itself, the festival, millions of people grooving together, beautiful.

The Festival trip. Strength in numbers. Quantity as a substitute for quality. There hasn't been a single one of the massive festivals, free or pay to enter, in which the whole incredible energy of pop culture hasn't been perverted and diverted, converted by an evil alchemical process into gold to pour into someone's pockets.

The Stones played in Hyde Park for free, and I was there, it was fairly beautiful, only partly because of the Stones (they played worse, probably, than at any other time in their career) but because there was a sense that we constituted a real, a viable alternative. The policemen and the ambulancemen were there by our permission and anyway we had our own fuzz, the Angels, and though it was rather rugged close up to the stage, with the young girls in their chiffon blouses mashing their little tits up against the crush barriers, pushed by the mass of people behind them, the sun shone and we lay in its light and ate yoghurt at non-ripoff prices and heard Mick read a verse or two of Shelley and watched the released butterflies flutter by in remembrance of Brian Jones, the one they'd found a few days before, lying in his pool like the hero of some Gloria Swanson movie, the one who'd lived that mythical 'fuck you' Stones lifestyle to the full and been broken by it, and been dropped when the break showed in his music. Still and all, it was free, which was the trip we were travelling back in 1968.

Free, nothing! The Stones made a fortune out of the rotten movie Jo Durden-Smith made of the event for Granada, a film which manages to over-emphasize the role the Stones had played at the concert and at the same time to include very little footage that told us anything more about where the Stones were at than any average Top of the Pops promo clip.

Altamont, which was the same story re-run as a horror movie in an alternative reality, where the Angels weren't our gentle-under-it-all British chapter but the genuine American fascist variety, mean and ugly and dirty as the years-old crud on their Originals, we will talk about later.

Isle of Wight. A true ripoff. An overnight slum where more effort was put into security (with guard dogs so savage they even bit their handlers) than into sanitation, for which the most apt symbol might well be a plastic-skinned Dayglo-pink parboiled Frankfurter.

The only thing was that it occurred at exactly the right time to spook Bob Dylan out of hiding, but if you listen to the bootleg you can hear just how badly he actually sang. But was anyone listening?

Then there was Woodstock, 'three days of peace, music and . . . love' (dig the elbow-nudging innuendo of the last word, because when a movie says love these days it always means fucking in one guise or another, in this case an actually rather beautiful scene taken with a long-focus lens peeping through shoulder-high grass at a couple making it right there, unaware that millions would be watching in movie houses for years afterwards). Time and the fact that Mike Wadleigh's very skilful movie grossed more than 'Sound of Music' (proving actually exactly what?) have glossed over the fact that Woodstock was an official disaster, like a hurricane or an earthquake, and that it became a free festival only because the alternative was to filter the people through the turnstiles as fast as possible, which was still so slow that most of them would have been left waiting for weeks after it ended.

The movie shows some of this, rather like a Sunday colour supplement feature on starvation in Pakistan, but what it doesn't show is that, thanks to the movie, the losses the organizers told the people about have turned into nice fat profits, so that some who jumped off the carousel a little too early in the game have gone into court demanding the right to climb back on again.

What people think about as Woodstock is Joni Mitchell's return to the garden in her song, but she wasn't even there 'in the shit from the overflowing latrines and the mud, she was safe on the West Coast.

Woodstock attracted, how many? A quarter of a million? The people in Toronto appear to have thought of a number, say a million, then they doubled it, and Lennon began to feel only slightly uneasy.

It's too simple to point a scornful finger at him and say it was obvious, by then a big festival of those proportions could only bring trouble to everyone involved in it, because what, really, does John Lennon know? He's been in a coccoon since the early 1960s. He's never been to a proper festival. Even if he went, would he unroll his bed in the mud with the rest of the freaks out there half a mile from the stage? He'd be grooving snug and safe in a VIP enclosure. He couldn't afford to be anywhere else.

This remoteness has inspired resentment among many who have been inspired by Jagger's flaunting in the face of authority, which got him busted for drugs long before any of the Beatles, though they did it as much as he. I remember a conversation I had with a couple of fairly well-known London heads after the police finally caught up with Lennon.

'Anyway,' said one, 'groovy. If there's one thing I was pleased about was seeing John Lennon get nicked. Then they won't put out any more B-sides like "Revolution". It's all about Don't come to us with your Revolution son, we don't want to know. Everything's pretty and flowery.

'The Beatles live within such a closed circle that they don't ever have to face the outside world, so they don't know what it's like. They've forgotten what the outside world's like. They used to know.

'Groovy, now John Lennon's got nicked. Now maybe they'll start facing up to the same sort of problems that every other freak in the country has to face.

'So they signed an advert in *The Times* for the legalizing of pot smoking. Big deal. Someone comes round to you with a form, we all smoke dope, saying legalize dope. Yeah yeah man, we'll sign.

'That doesn't give them the slightest bit of insight into the paranoia: Is that knock on the door a groovy trendy psychedelic friend or the local friendly neighbour-hood fuzz coming to kick shit out of me and nick me. They don't face that. Now maybe they will.'

I wonder if he realized exactly how unrealistic he was being, I mean was it deliberate? When he suddenly freaked the organizers that time in Denmark, telling them he'd decided the festival should be 'free entry for a dollar', that's about 43p, decimal currency.

Originally they'd planned on exactly 25 times that sum; then they'd come down to fifteen dollars for the three days. It would have been difficult to have made it less, even if they didn't do what Lennon had promised on his flying visit to Toronto and made sure that everyone got paid a fair day's wage. Just setting up the event, with stages and decent sound, and not forgetting the latrines, would cost about a million dollars.

When a troupe of festival organizers came to San Francisco in late February to enlist the support of the Jefferson Airplane and the West Coast heads for the event, the contradictions began to become evident. The Festival would be free, they said, and tickets would cost fifteen dollars. *Huh?* And a big fence would keep out Hells Angels and other undesirables so that there was no repetition of Altamont. *Wow!* There was no mention at that stage of barbed wire entanglements and machine gun towers and searchlights.

And the bands? Well, *er*, anyone who wanted to could come and play, but basically what would happen was the top hip people in the world would be asked to name their favourite bands and *that* would be the bill. A dictatorship of the hip meritocracy. Furthermore, people from the moon (actually, they live *inside* the moon, which is why the US astronauts have missed them so far) would definitely be coming. And only positive music would be permitted, avoiding Altamont again, though the Stones would be very welcome if they came.

And they were planning on six million people now.

This bullshit, bear in mind, they were laying on the real pros of the business, people like Chip Monk who knew about festivals. And they knew about the magic and religion freaks like the Harbinger cult as well. They had them on their doorstep, right there in California.

It is hard to believe, as I have said, that Lennon hadn't already realized what was evident to everyone outside the hallowed inner circle: that the festival, as so far planned, just couldn't happen, or if it did, it would be a disaster of Biafran proportions.

After the meeting, Jon Carroll wrote in *Rolling Stone*: 'Almost everybody wants the peace festival to succeed, but the taste of disaster was too fresh. At a time when John Lennon wanted to press the great crusade ever forward, the veterans of Altamont wanted to rethink a few assumptions, to see if there's not a better way to get where everybody wants to go. And the Toronto people were so vague about so many important questions, so apparently unaware of the magnitude of what they were proposing, that many found it hard to put aside their doubts and follow.'

John Lennon included. He had Allen Klein announce that he would only participate if the whole thing were free, if all the profits went to the projected Peace Foundation to be administered by John Lennon and his accountants, and if Lennon had complete artistic control, with the title of director. Whether John Brower or any of the others would have anything to do with it, when and if it took place, seemed problematical, to say the least.

Lennon himself went further. After he received reports of the San Francisco meeting, and a specific report from John Brower on the way things were shaping, he cabled his immediate dissociation: 'Have read your report. You have done exactly what we told you not to. We told you we wanted it to be free. We want nothing to do with you or your festival. Please do not use our name or our ideas or symbols.

'Yours in disgust, John and Yoko.'

He also wrote a special article on the subject for the next issue of *Rolling Stone* which must have been some diatribe in the original. Allen Klein spent five days taking out the libels before he could release it, too late for the April 2 issue of the magazine.

It would be interesting to see the uncensored version, not only for the full unattenuated Lennon going at full blast, but also because as Lennon recalls it now the article was apparently not confined to Toronto, but also blasted off on something else that was bugging him more than somewhat, namely the reaction of Beatledom to Yoko.

In a much later interview with Jann Wenner (published in *Rolling Stone* in January 1971, reprinted in *Club* magazine in May and June of that year and no doubt elsewhere round the world; it was a very good, a very frank interview) John was unburdening himself on the other Beatles' attitude to Yoko and he said suddenly: 'I was always hoping that they would come round. I couldn't believe it, and they all sat there with their wives, like a fucking jury, and the only thing I did was write that piece (*Rolling Stone*, April 17,

1970) about "some of our *beast* friends" in my usual way – because I was never honest enough, I always had to write in that gobbly-gook – and that's what they did to us.'

Now Lennon's memory may be at fault, but the reference in brackets, giving the date of the issue, was put in by the editors who presumably had a chance to check, and the only article by John Lennon in that issue is a piece exclusively about Toronto under the head 'Have We All Forgotten What Vibes Are?' The words 'some of our *beast* friends' do not appear anywhere in that issue.

This is not so irrelevant as you might think, because if John was still sounding off about Yoko in a piece on Toronto, it tells you something about the way his mind was working then, the general paranoia.

Most of the article is about John Brower not doing what he was told. The Harbinger people got to John by way of his friend, 'Dr' Zee Hamrick, it's true, and John's idea was they should go to Canada with Brower 'to keep his "vibes" steady. We still hoped that the larger concept of the Peace Festival and its *karmic effects* on the world had lifted him out of the *bread hangup scene* and he would turn on to being a *peace promoter*.'

However, after meeting the two proposed 'overseers' from Harbinger, John decided not to use them 'as they looked like they would confuse the issue even more. (The spokesman was a magician who was going to turn anyone who messed up the Festival into a frog or something.)'

As so often happens with him, that provincial spirit of Liverpudlian incredulousness seems to have come to his aid at that moment, but not before time.

'In spite of everything,' he concluded, 'and you haven't heard *half* – Yoko and I would still like to be part of a Peace Festival in Canada or anywhere else. Our latest idea was to have everyone at the Festival singing only Hari Krishna – including all those famous stars I'm supposed to be getting in touch with whom I'm sure will run a mile if I call them now. . . .'

Six million people singing a mantra! It was more conceptual art. The last time anything at all on that scale had been managed was at Nurenberg before the war, and the words were 'Sieg Heil'. But we digress.

The final paragraphs of the article deserve quoting at length: 'Someone said, "Do we need a Festival?" Yoko and I still think we need it, not just to show that we can gather peacefully and groove to rock bands, but to change the balance of energy power. On earth and, therefore, in the universe.

'Have we all forgotten what vibes are? Can you imagine what we could do together in one spot – thinking – singing – and praying for Peace – one million souls apart from any TV link-ups etc to the rest of the planet. If we came together for *one reason*, we could *make it together*!

'We need help! – It is out of our control – Brower does not represent us any more than you do – all we have is our name – (Klein will help any way we want but he won't let us be hyped) we are sorry for the confusion, it's bigger than both of us – we are doing our best for all our sakes – we still believe – pray for us.

'Love and Peace.

'John and Yoko.'

The telegraphese Mayday distress signal tone of the end has a sinking ship air to it that cannot have escaped Lennon, consummate artist that he is in the use of words.

The response in Toronto was more prosaic.

A press release from Karma Productions read: 'John and Yoko Lennon are no longer involved with the Toronto Peace Festival, planned for July 3, 4 and 5 at Mosport Park. But the Festival will proceed as planned. . . .

'John and Yoko now want the Festival to be completely free, and while we agree with the intent, we are not prepared to accept the responsibility.

'Imagine what would happen if two million people arrived from all over North America and from countries outside this continent, only to find that the physical surroundings limited the maximum audience to 200,000. We find it difficult to believe that so many people would simply return to their homes without being emotionally upset.'

Pointing out that on December 17 of the previous year, John Lennon had said everyone would get paid, the release continued: 'We don't understand this sudden switch which renders the whole idea of a festival logistically impossible. There is no such thing as something for nothing ... not even a Peace Festival.'

So the figure had come down to 200,000 (rather less than at Woodstock) and in fact with no acts yet booked and only two months to go that was pretty optimistic. Too optimistic, in fact; the Fesitval never took place.

Now, it is rather too easy to blame John Brower's 'bread hang-up' for what went wrong, for someone somewhere has to find the money for the sound system, the stage, the transport, and those inevitable latrines, and my experience is that people who are good at that are not always the nicest people to know simply *because* they are good at it. Rock musicians are mostly nicer people to know because they are bad at it, which is why I number rather more rock musicians among my friends than millionaires (though I know a few). Anything that operates within the money system, whether it's Apple or a festival or a tanner church hall jumble sale or even a publishing house producing revolutionary propaganda, is going to get thrown off course to a lesser or greater degree to the exact extent that money is a consideration to it.

They crucified John Brower, a man I have never met, and perhaps he deserved it, but the words these radically chic media men use presuppose such a basically Tolstoyan unconcern with anything so basic as 'bread hangups' that it comes as something of a surprise to learn that they appeared in a magazine that is such a hot little profitable property that Hugh Hefner has been trying to buy it for his bunny warren: 'And the shuck goes on ... the point is that Brower has constantly asked for trust and love from people who, against the enormous paranoia of the world at large, have been attempting to maintain those virtues. So Brower got a lot of trust and love – and proceeded, it seems now, to exploit it. Long hair and dope smoking are no longer enough – it's turned from a movement into a market, and half the world wants to cash in.

'Would you buy a used car from John Brower?'

Actually, I wouldn't buy a car, used or otherwise, from anybody because like money, the car is obsolescent, if indeed we ever needed it. That's much how I feel about money. But occasionally I hire cars. And like John Lennon and the editors of *Rolling Stone*, I have to have money to pay for them, and also to pay my grocer and my landlord, though I probably like it rather less than they do. Not because it is somehow idealistically dirty: if money soils my hands, the grime is metaphorical rust from a device that originated in a Mediterranean society decaying out of classlessness centuries before the birth of Christ, and not because of any of this ethical bull whose main effect is to fit us even more snugly into the money system, because it hangs us up with personalities instead of going for root causes.

From where I sit, two things and two things only distinguish Toronto from any other festivals, actual or projected, successful or unsuccessful: the highly publicized incompetence of the people trying to get it together, and the ubiquitous presence of a personality like Lennon, with or without his ideas, and whether or not they were practical.

As it happens, I've been involved in one or two festivals myself. I helped to set up the basic financial arrangements for a very similar event planned for Britain (in that the Beatles, the Stones and Presley were all named as definite certainties) and I've been close enough to the power centres of most of the other major European festivals to know that, whatever peace and love the organizers may give the masses from the platform, it's strictly a financial affair when the chips are down. Always. All ways.

This particular one came to me by way of Sam Cutler, then something important in Stones management, who had heard I might be able to point him in the general direction of the money to get a festival going, though God knows I've little enough of it myself. However, I do know a few millionaires as I've said (mainly through my tailor) so I put Sam in touch with one. Eventually I found myself setting up a meeting: plus Cutler and myself there was an ex-pirate radio tycoon, a trendy Lord (who roared up on a 1,000 cc Honda you could hear a block away), one or two hip media people, mainly records and TV, and indeed most of the hipocrats of London who pulled any weight would have been exterminated if the Square Brigade had tossed a grenade through the open window. Professionals, all, and the way they carved up the action – you do the programmes, you have the hotdogs concession, you have the recording rights, you can film – down to every last farthing impressed me with the realization that this, at the end, was what the 'underground' really amounted to, a bunch of guys in a smokefilled room carving up a million quid cake. I've been in similar situations when it's been Havana Havana smoke, when the businessmen have been short-haired straights, buying and selling textiles, say, or planning an advertising programme, and I've been there when it's been pot smoke and me the only guy in the room not turning on, and the heads are planning a festival or launching a new underground newspaper, and believe me the smell is much the same in the long run.

As a matter of record, they got their £1 million (not from my millionaire, as it happened) but the day after Altamont they lost it again. That particular festival never took place.

The point of this is that if the negotiations had been conducted in the same public gaze as was Toronto, and if a top pop figure had been around all the time, intoning the same well-meaning platitudes the while, *Rolling Stone* might have had some similarly hard words to say about us. Deservedly, perhaps.

Today (that is, in the summer of 1971) John Lennon has taken to wearing a little red Mao badge, though as recently as December 1969 he'd told a press conference: 'I'd go to Russia, but I'd think twice about China.' Radical politics now seems to be taking the place in the space in his heart left by religion, which he dismisses as 'Godshit' though it's a mistake to see this new commitment as something entirely new in his thinking.

As Lennon points out, there were actually two versions of 'Revolution' with exactly opposite messages, reflecting his own confusion at the time. The one which was released on the back of the 'Hey Jude' single was the very gentle 'count me out' song which upset the radicals, while on the white album the much tougher, harder rocking version with different words to the same tune is, he says, the original. And it says 'count me in'.

'I put in both because I wasn't sure,' he told Tariq Ali in an interview for *Red Mole*. 'On the version released as a single I said "when you talk about destruction you can count me out". I didn't want to get killed. I didn't really know that much about the Maoists, but I just knew that they seemed to be so few and yet they painted themselves green and stood in front of the police waiting to get picked off. I thought the original Communist revolutionaries co-ordinated themselves a bit better and didn't go around shouting about it. That was how I felt – I was really asking a question, as someone from the working class, even though I was playing the capitalist game.'

That's what he's doing all the time, right now, asking questions. After years of remoteness, sealed off from the media almost as hermetically as Dylan, Lennon is suddenly

... *accessible* to the right sort of interviewer, and often he makes it quite plain that he vill ask ze qvestions:

Yoko: ... The Establishment likes people who take no responsibility and cannot respect themselves.

Red Mole: I suppose workers' control is about that.

John: Haven't they tried out something like that in Yugoslavia, they are free of the Russians? I'd like to go there and see how it works.

Red Mole: Well, they have, they did try to break with the Stalinist pattern. But instead of allowing uninhibited workers' control, they added a strong dose of political bureaucracy ...

John: It seems that all revolutions end up with a personality cult – even the Chinese seem to need a father-figure. I expect this happens in Cuba too with Che and Fidel. ... In Western-style Communism we would have to create an almost imaginary workers' image of *themselves* as the father-figure.

Red Mole: That's a pretty cool idea – the working class becomes its own Hero. ...

Yoko: The people have got to trust in themselves.

Red Mole: That's the vital point. The working class must be instilled with a feeling of confidence in itself. This can't be done just by propaganda – the workers must move, take over their own factories and tell the capitalists to bugger off. This is what began to happen in May 1968 in France ... the workers began to feel their own strength.

John: But the Communist Party wasn't up to that, was it?

Red Mole: No, they weren't.

I have deliberately abbreviated the remarks from *Red Mole*, keeping John and Yoko's contributions in their entirety, because otherwise it is hard to remember exactly who is interviewing whom.

John takes as much political blah from Tariq and his co-interviewer as he has done in the past from the evangelists of various other religions and magics, but that

H

doesn't necessarily mean he's fooled. He may let on soon that he knew all along they were threatening to turn us into frogs.

For instance, it provokes no outburst from Tariq Ali, currently a Trotskyist, when John puts down the *Morning Star*, because it's OK to criticize the CP Establishment, though the same strictures could apply with equal validity to *Red Mole*, because they proceed from the same basic assumptions about the development of the state which Marx developed in the hey-day of the industrial capitalist age, claming merely that as Trots they are closer to the pure spirit of basic unadulterated Marxism-Leninism. 'I keep reading the *Morning Star*,' says John at one point, 'to see if there's any hope; it seems to be written for dropped-out middle-aged liberals.' A valid judgement; what he thinks of *Red Mole* he doesn't say.

Yoko tries to examine the different role of violence in a society with mass communications, an interesting concept that deserves careful consideration, and she's interrupted with a tired old Marxist bromide trotted out as a convenient excuse for not rethinking anything: 'No ruling class in the whole of history has given up power voluntarily and I don't see that changing.'

Just for a moment, let's listen to Yoko. Like all the other trendies, *Red Mole* seemed to tend to dismiss what she says as the dreams of an idealistic crank, but they are worth studying more carefully. I have omitted *Red Mole's* interjections (that's all they are) to preserve the flow of her argument, but not John's, because though he takes a fairly classic radical position on violence, at least he responds spontaneously to what she is saying.

Yoko: We are very lucky really, because we can create our own reality, John and me, but we know the important thing is to communicate with other people.

John: The more reality we face, the more we realize that unreality is the main programme of the day. The more real we become, the more abuse we take, so it does radicalize us in a way. But it would be better if there were more of us.

Yoko: We mustn't be traditional in the way we communicate with people – especially with the Establishment. We should surprise people by saying new things in an entirely new way. Communications of that sort can have a fantastic power so long as you don't do only what they expect you to do.

I get very sad when I think about Vietnam where there seems to be no choice but violence. This violence goes on for centuries, perpetuating itself. In the present age, when communication is so rapid, we should create a different tradition, traditions are created every day. Five years now is like a hundred years before. We are living in a society that has no history. There's no precedent for this kind of society so we can break the old patterns.

... violence isn't just a conceptual thing, you know. I saw a programme about this kid who had come back from Vietnam – he'd lost his body from the waist down. He was just a lump of meat, and he said: 'Well, I guess it was a good experience.'

John: He didn't want to face the truth, he didn't want to think it had all been a waste....

Yoko: But think of the violence, it could happen to your kids...

... in a way the new music showed things could be transformed by new channels of communication.

John: Yes, but as I said, nothing really changed.

Yoko: Well, something changed and it was for the better. All I'm saying is that perhaps we can make a revolution without violence.

John: But you can't take power without struggle.

Because when it comes to the nitty gritty they won't let the people have any power, they'll give all the rights to perform and to dance for them, but no real power...

Yoko: The thing is, even after the revolution if people

don't have any trust in themselves, they'll get new problems.

Right on, Yoko!

The beautiful thing about this exchange is that it is a true dialogue. Though at the time Yoko is putting forth one idea, espousing non-violence basically from a pragmatic point of view rather than merely expressing an emotional pacifism (but she doesn't make the mistake of trying to control her emotions, either) and John is taking an opposite line, they are working something out between them.

In contrast, you can take any one of *Red Mole's* interjections and put it anywhere you like, it doesn't matter, and it contributes nothing, answers nothing, raises no new questions, suggests no new answers: 'Popular violence against their oppressors is always justified. It cannot be avoided.'

That's a view which hasn't changed since the Nineteenth Century, the era of the machine and the industrial factory which created Marxism, a time when the most sophisticated computer in existence was Babbage's cumbersome though brilliant affair of gears and wheels, mechanical not electronic.

The Nineteenth Century was an age of great individuals, which is why the greatest philosophical contribution the Victorians made to the world was Marxism, with its personality cults – Lenin, Stalin, Trotsky, Mao. Because we live in an electronic age, these heroes are as irrelevant to the needs of today as Lennon sees the Beatles to be.

In his innocence, Lennon is willing to accept that, possibly, Russia might need a Stalin, China a Mao, Cuba a Fidel, but when he leaves the realm of theorizing and comes home to the place he knows from his own experience, Britain, he knows better and he comes up with an idea that's not quite so novel as *Red Mole* seems to find it: the people as their own image. 'Everybody is a leader.' (Toronto, December 1969.)

The 'Sections' which ruled Paris from 1790 and which started the French Revolution consisted of the entire population, meeting in permanent session at the Hotel de Ville every evening. It was only after the Revolution that the less direct methods of deputized rule were substituted, as the French bourgeoisie consolidated its power.

Lennon's politics have always been the sort of thinking that the politicos despise, for good reason, for if people rely upon their own experience they will put the politicians out of business. Lennon's are the instinctive reaction of someone who *knows* things have got to change, drawing upon the heritage of the underground movement his class have conducted against the system for centuries: 'I've always been politically minded, you know, and against the status quo. It's pretty basic when you're brought up, like I was, to hate and fear the police as a natural enemy and to despise the army as something that takes everybody away and leaves them dead somewhere. I mean, it's just a basic working class thing, though it begins to wear off when you get older, get a family and get swallowed up in the system. In my case I've never not been political, though religion tended to overshadow it in my acid days; that would be around '65 or '66. And that religion was directly the result of all that superstar shit – religion was an outlet for my repression. I thought, "Well, there's someting else to life, isn't there? This isn't it, surely?" But I was always political in a way, you know. In the two books I wrote even though they were written in a sort of Joycean gobbledegook, there's many knocks at religion and there is a play about a worker and a capitalist. I've been satirizing the system since my childhood. I used to write magazines in school and hand them around. I was very conscious of class, they would say with a chip on my shoulder, because I knew what happened to me and I knew about the class repression coming down on us – it was a fucking fact but in the hurricane Beatle world it got left out – I got farther away from reality for a time.

What is hard for Lennon to realize is that the political trip is unreal too, at least the way it is played by H. Wilson and E. Heath and J. Gollan and T. Ali and L. Brezhnev. That is basically what went wrong at Toronto, it was an outmoded political trip of that kind, the thought that being John and Yoko gave them some sort of special power to achieve what Mr and Mrs John Nameless couldn't do, the failure to realize that being John and Yoko was precisely what *disqualified* them from the start, what made it such a bummer all the way through.

Better to do like Mick Jagger, to write it in your songs and listen carefully to every appeal for cash whether it comes from Release or the Angry Brigade and give when your instincts tell you to give and only then, and if you must go, prowl round the edges of the demos unrecognized and try your best to understand because, being Mick or John or Bobbie or even Joanie, what actually else can you do without fucking up the whole scene? At very best you can hope to be a Daniel Cohn-Bendit, and Danny had the sense to vote for his own deposition when it became clear the media were building up a personality cult round him to make him an instrument of counter-revolution. So far there's no news of a similar move from Mao or Fidel, but we're waiting in hopes.

The electronic maharishi has pointed out many times that the switch from machines to electronic devices as the prime movers for change within the community means a corresponding change from individualism to the collective, and this means that the division of the people into warring factions (the root word of 'democracy', demos, 'means properly a division' says the classical scholar George Thompson in 'Aeschylus and Athens', page 193) is obsolete.

'In our software world of instant electric communications movement,' McLuhan told *Playboy* in March 1969, 'politics is shifting from the old patterns of political representation by electoral delegation to a new form of spontaneous and instantaneous communal involvement in all areas of decision making.' It's a more high-flown way of saying what Yoko told *Red Mole*.

In Toronto in December of that same year, John Lennon was telling *McLuhan*, and CBC TV was televizing the whole event to bring in the global family: 'We are all told we aren't artists and poets and musicians round about when we're 11 years old when they try to syphon us off. But we're all artists and poets and musicians until somebody says we're not. . . .

'Language and song is to me, apart from being pure vibrations, just like trying to describe a dream. And because we don't have telepathy or whatever it is, we try to describe the dream to each other, to verify to each other, what we believe is inside each other . . . we can't say it. No matter how you say it, it's never how you want to say it. . . .

'As soon as you find the pattern, you break it. Otherwise it gets boring . . .

'Because it's always searching for the ultimate, and each pattern or format you find is another little trip off the side. A spin off. . . .

'The Beatles pattern is one that has to be scrapped. Because if it remains the same it's a monument or a museum and one thing this age is about is no museums. And the Beatles turned into a museum so they have to be scrapped or deformed or changed. . . .'

(We are moving towards) 'Just complete freedom: and non-expectation from audience or musician or performer. Just complete freedom. And then when we've had that for a few hundred years, then we can talk about playing around with patterns and bars and music again. We must get away from the patterns we've had for these thousands of years.'

John Lennon knows, right down to the DNA in his cells, what it is all about, which is why when he drops all pretences and lets it come out unaided, almost, as on 'John

Lennon: Plastic Ono Band' the result is just about the most political rock and roll record since the earlier Chuck Berrys. For one thing, because it is so *personal* ('a mass society in which personal diversity is encouraged while at the same time everybody reacts and interacts simultaneously to every stimulus' is where McLuhan says we are going).

'Working Class Hero' is a bitter look at superstardom:

'There's room at the top they are telling you still
But first you must learn how to smile as you kill
If you want to be like the folks on the hill
A working class hero is something to be.
'. . . If you want to be a hero well just follow me.'

In 'I Found Out', the image of stardom is linked with the recurring theme of parental abandonment:

'I heard something 'bout my ma and my pa
They didn't want me so they made me a star.' –

Probably the most important song on the entire album, 'God', is a very positive statement, in spite of or even because of the long string of negatives in the middle:

'I don't believe in magic . . . in I-Ching . . . Bible . . .
Tarot . . . Hitler . . . Jesus . . . Buddha . . Mantra . . . Gita
. . . Yoga . . . Kings . . . Elvis . . . Zimmerman . . . Beatles.

'I just believe in me
Yoko and me
And that's reality.'

As Billy Preston's gospel-tinged piano tinkles the same sort of flourishes you'd expect to hear behind a Mahalia Jackson spiritual, he says farewell to the dream without regret, and farewell to Paul's scrambled eggs as well:

'Yesterday
I was the dreamweaver
But now I'm reborn
I was the walrus
But now I'm John
And so dear friends
You just have to carry on
The dream is over.'

You just have to carry on. Because John Lennon's not going to be a Messiah, thank God, and we've got to do it for ourselves. Like the spiritual says:

'You've got to go down that lonesome valley,
You've got to go there for yourself.
Ain't nobody else can go there for you.
You've got to go, Lord, you've got to go.'

His songs say it. And that's his job. Messiahs are, in comparison with poets, rather too thick on the ground these days.

VII

Freaking the Media

"aretha, pegged by choir boys & other pearls of mamas as too gloomy a much of witchy & dont you know no happy songs"
    —*Tarantula (bootleg edition)*

THE FIRST time I met Bobbie Dylan, I was trying to interview him for a Partyline Marxist publication, me thinking he was still in that revolutionary Hattie Carroll-Hollis Brown Masters of War bag.

'Tell me, Mr Dallas,' said he, 'are you for me or against me?' drinking wine from a paper cup.

Then Al Grossman's mafia hustled me out into the hallway backstage at the Royal Festival Hall before I had time to mumble much more than 'Well, I hardly know you.' Or as he himself tells a student interviewer in 'Don't Look Back': 'I don't have an attitude towards you at all. Why should I have an attitude towards you? I don't even know you.'

I put it down to paranoia, because by then he was already running into plenty of static. No longer the darling of the east coast People's Songs set, though Sis Cunningham and the boys of Broadside still had some inkling of where Blind Boy Grunt was at. 'Bob Dylan doesn't know his ethno-musicology' was the much-quoted New York graffito scrawled by some smart aleck kid who'd just stumbled upon Cousin Emmie playing her rubber glove when there was Bobbie, the Jewish boy from Minnesota, playing Chuck Berry's 'Too Much Monkey Business' as if he were the Beatles, plugging himself into the energy of electric Africa, 'Subterranean Homesick Blues', the speed king jive-talking slice of urban American street life that took half a decade for all of us petit bourgeois leftists to tune into, we were so busy telling ourselves it was more unintelligible than 'Heartbreak Hotel', with less rhyme and syntax, if such a thing were possible.

Paranoia would have been excusable, I suppose, but it took me a while to suss how gently Dylan had been putting me on, giving me that 'who is not for me is against me' jive straight out of my textbook revolutionaries' mouths, the interviewer stumped by the unanswerable question. It was a special application of Dylan's favourite game. Freaking the media.

In those days you were polite to pressmen if you were in showbiz. You'd better. I made you and by God I can break you, as Cecil B. de Mille once said to Jehovah.

These days, the rock poets have learned to play the media along in ways that keep them always on the defensive. I was there once when a journalist asked Jim Morrison if his sexy come-on on stage was just a pose, or did he really feel that horny?

'Well,' said Jim with great seriousness after a moment's thought, 'it's like when you get up in the morning and have to decide whether to wear the blue suit or the brown suit.'

That is the game. You don't refuse to answer the question but you answer in such a way that if you're not hip the reply leaves more questions unanswered than before. I mean, look into Morrison's reply and it *is* an answer to what was, let's face it, a pretty dumb remark. An answer of sorts, posed in exactly the terms that your average straight newsman ought to be able to understand. If, that is, he was able to stand outside and look at himself.

Morrison's answer re-poses the question at a more general level: when we choose our clothes for the day, when we try to make the girls in the audience wet their knickers with unsublimated desire, when we put on the right face to ask the boss for a rise, to get a girl into bed, stop a traffic warden from giving us a ticket, explain to the wife what it was exactly about tonight's drink with the boys that made it last until 3 a.m., when we play any of the elaborate rituals that make up the game of life, what is pose and what is natural? If a man is a natural poseur, it is an affectation for him to act natural.

And anyway a pop musician's world is so plumb unnatural, in straight media terms anyway, that when the newsman tries to interpret what he learns, he gets the whole thing so arse-about-face that the only result is to increase the mutual misunderstanding and suspicion between them.

Partly this is a basic problem in communications, upon which people like Chomsky and Colin Cherry have pronounced at length. In one of his rare serious press confrontations, shown on San Francisco's KQED TV station at the end of 1965, Dylan tried to grapple with it: 'I just know in my mind that we all have a different idea of all the words we're using. Like, if I say the word "house", like we're both going to see a different house. If I just say the word, right? So we're using all these other words like "mass production" and "movie magazine" and we all have a different idea of these words, too, so I don't even know what we're saying.'

Like all establishments with their organizational roots in the print-based technology of the industrial era – which includes the money corporations which control the big record companies and other electronic mass media – the press always tries to reinterpret what they find in pop culture in terms which they themselves can understand.

Hence the whole superstar trip, something which is in essence completely alien to it, a means by which the Nineteenth Century tries to come to terms with the Twentyfirst.

In that same televised press conference, an obviously well-meaning reporter tried to draw Dylan out on the subject of his own vast popularity, to his own frustration and the increasing bafflement of his subject, to whom the questions were as incomprehensible as they were irrelevant.

'Well, what do you want me to say about it?' asked Dylan eventually.

Interviewer: You seem almost embarrassed to admit you're popular.

Dylan: Well, I'm not embarrassed, I mean, you know, well what do you want, exactly, for me to say? You want me to jump up and say 'Hallelujah!' and crash the cameras or do something weird? Tell me. Tell me. I'll go along with you. If I can't go along with you, I'll find somebody to go along with you.'

Pressing the point, the interviewer asked him if he thought he was popular because audiences identified themselves with him, but Dylan could only honestly say: 'I have no idea. I don't really come too much in contact.'

That was true. During the enforced rest that followed his motor cycle accident he was to point out that despite his isolation he actually met more people than he did when touring. However, said the TV interviewer, this reply would disappoint the people (meaning, as media people always mean when they speak disparagingly of the tastes and aspirations of the public, that he himself would be disappointed).

'Oh well,' said Dylan, his patience visibly fraying, 'I don't want to disappoint anybody. I mean, tell me what I should say. You know, I'll certainly go along with anything but I really don't have too much of an idea.'

One of the problems is the newsman's need to put things

into words which are exclusive rather than inclusive, a hang-up which is even more severe when the newsman is a critic, a journalist attempting to assume the mantle of the great literary critics of the past, in an area where this 'high art' approach is the greatest anachronism of all. The critics' tendency to look for 'art' as the justification for anything (currently even in reggae, one of the most practical, functional and journeyman-honest musics since the Renaissance screwed us up) has had more adverse effect upon the good health of popular music than any single factor outside the involvement of accountants who have been put into the most creative companies by the corporations in control.

Having their growth in the period when all human activities were becoming more and more fragmented (an alienation which began, in many ways, with the earliest division between artist and audience, as a special application of the god-man, king-subjects, priest-congregation split which had preceded it in the long history of the break-up of the human community) the critics based their writings upon a fragmented view of the arts which makes nonsense of the total field effect of most modern culture. Hence we have seen acres of newsprint devoted to such non-questions as the attempts to define jazz, folk music, or pop and rock, treating such forms as if they were static *things* rather than dynamic processes, descriptions of the changing three-fold relationship between the creator and his creation, and those who observe the act of creation, who are gradually (but at a rate of increasing acceleration) changing from the role of passive observers to active participants, a transition which is actively resisted by most critics, and also by those creators who are fool enough to pay any attention to what they say.

So all rock musicians know, at least at an instinctive level, that all meetings with critics can only be to a greater or lesser extent exercises in mutual frustration, where differences in the basic use of the vocabulary are so profound that the musician is rather in the position of a person explaining the colour of a rose to someone blind from birth. For the concept that the average critic associates with music is as abstract, and as unrelated to the sheer physical effort of getting up on a stage in front of the thousand watt amps to be a popular musician, as that blind man's idea of what colour means. Even if you were able, by reducing the matter perhaps to the mathematical question of the wavelengths of the various lightwaves, to help the blind man obtain at least an intellectual understanding of the relation of 'red' to 'green', of the emotions inspired by the infinite gradations from rose pink to scarlet possible in a single bud he would have not the slightest conception. The best pop critics are in a position of a man who has got as far as digging what red means, in terms of wavelength. But they are still basically blind.

In pop, where few critics have any real musical training of any kind, even including the largely irrelevant traditions of post-Renaissance harmonic music, they often overcome the lack by an abstruse kind of nit-picking, which musicians find particularly irritating. They are for ever trying to divide up the performers into separate, watertight compartments, then turning to savage those who dare to cross these completely arbitrary boundaries: 'What business has a soul singer performing folk rock?' they will ask in horror. Or better still, they will invent a new hybrid category to account for the constant cross-fertilization which is such a feature of modern pop: psychedelic rock, rock-and-soul, afro-rock, folk-jazz and the like.

Is it any wonder that when people ask Dylan what bag *he* is in, he is likely to reply: 'Oh I think of myself more as a song and dance man.' This really freaks them, because if they know anything at all (and so few of them really do) they know, or think they know, that the one thing Dylan has nothing to do with is that old soft shoe ballin' the jack routine, and then he comes on singing 'Blue Moon' or the Beatles re-stage a Busby Berkley spectacular complete with glass staircase ('Your Mother Should Know') as the climax to their Magical Mystery Home Movie, and the critics have to try and puzzle it all out, confused.

But it is not merely confusion, for Dylan was saying something highly relevant about the current state of the art in 1965 when he rated the Sir Douglas Quintet, an averagely good AM-station rock band, as one of the best upcoming groups of folk singers, as 'the best that are going to have a chance of reaching the commercial airways'.

This is what upsets the media, this impossibility of distinguishing with any certainty when they are being put on, coupled with the slow realization that most of the time they are being simultaneously told the exact, literal truth and having their pissers pulled.

When Dylan says the message of his songs, basically, is 'good luck', the critics smile like people who are in on the gag, because can this be the bitter cynic whose 'It's Alright Ma I'm Only Bleeding' is such a devastating portrayal of American society with its claws unsheathed, as seen by the alienated and betrayed young? But indeed Dylan often says exactly that, as he insists: Good luck, I hope you make it. 'It's Alright Ma' ends with the words *it's life and life only* and 'Bob Dylan's 115th Dream' actually uses those words at the end of the last verse: *I just said good luck*.

The basic problem with pop culture is that it is a thing in transition, the music of a working class intelligentsia which has been bourgeoisified by the brainwashing systems of the universities and other educational institutions such as discotheques, cinemas and fashion boutiques. This audience tries all the time to fit what it hears into the literary critical petit bourgeois world view that has been forced upon them as the outlook of the cultured, educated man. They actually begin to believe that the critical categories mean anything more than a convenience to the compilers of indexes, so that in order to find an audience the performer has to conform to boundaries which have

I

no meaning to him or, in reality, to anyone else, and let him beware if he thinks that fame has given him the license to define his work in terms which owe their relevance to himself alone, and not to some sacred tablets brought down from Sinai by the bearded prophets of *Sing Out!* or their short-haired colleagues on *Billboard*.

Dylan started as a rock performer, singing Buddy Holly songs for fun long before he met Woody Guthrie (and indeed, by the time he did meet the great old man, Woody was really too ill with chorea in Greystone Hospital, New Jersey, to be able to convey anything meaningful musically to him). The first record he ever made was playing blues harmonica with Big Joe Williams, but since he came to the notice of the East Coast liberal-Marxist establishment in the person of John Hammond, Columbia's resident progressive jazz-folk-blues expert ('From Spirituals to Swing') and Director of Talent Acquisition, when Bobbie was playing on a session with Carolyn Hester, one of the first of the long-haired Greenwich Village-out-of-Rive-Gauche folk chanteuses to make it, he got himself labelled as folk.

Already then the mythic characters had become stereotypes. If you were a chick you had to be a homespun sort of bluestocking, a cross between Heloise and the average homesteader's gingham-clad wife in a John Ford western, long preferably blonde hair, so straight it looked as if she ironed it every night (and she probably did). She would sing in a rather expressionless, 'pure' style sounding like a fantasy of a milkmaid's voice, actually with its roots in New England schools' interpretation of madrigals, with more of the tonelessness of a castrated male counter-tenor than of the biting bagpipe tones of the true American country singer whom they claimed to emulate.

The young men had a more immediately folkier image, most of the trappings of which are still with us: the Dallas Airport hand-tooled leather boots, the bathtub-shrunk and bleached jeans by Levi Strauss (but never the actual button-fly baggy pants Levi still sell to cowpokes who'd chafe their balls off in the saddle with anything as tight as the normal citybilly's Levis), the shaggy General Custer hair joined a little later by the drooping Wyatt Earp moustache, a voice that told of duststorm-dried Mid-West wastes, and a lifestyle that was by Jack Kerouac out of Will Rogers.

She was the lady left in the locked tower by the old lord off to the Crusades, letting the young man with the duplicate key to her chastity belt climb up her yellow hair. He was the hobo, the footloose bum with a girl across the tracks from every freightyard, his thumb sunburned from cross-Continental hitching, his bootheels wandering down the pathbeaten trails from one coffeebar to the next.

As Jim Morrison said, choosing the role you'd play was a lot like choosing the clothes you wore. Often the clothes were all there was to it.

Bob Zimmerman, the bookish Jewish drop-out from Minnesota University who changed his name to Dylan in honour of dear dead boozy garrulous podgy old Dylan Thomas, found his role ready-made and broken-in for him by another Jewish boy, son of a Brooklyn doctor, a middleclass kid with bad vision who changed his name from Charles Elliott Adnopoz, first to Buck Elliott when he was trying to get into rodeos, then to Jack Elliott, a young man of whom Woody Guthrie had said with some justification, 'He sings more like me than I do'. It was from Jack that Dylan – and for that matter, Woody's own son Arlo, who was barely out of rompers when Woody went into hospital for the last time in 1954 – learnt the Okie croak which became his hallmark, which was ironic, since Bob the Zimmerman's origins were rather closer in spirit and slightly closer, even, in geography to Oklahoma than Elliott the Adnopoz's Brooklyn. He also borrowed Jack's talent for fantasy. When Jack came to England for the first time as deckhand on a luxury yacht, he told everyone he came from Oklahoma, and since then his stories of rambling round with Woody have become so mutually contradictory that possibly only Marjorie, Guthrie's wife who kept closely in touch with her ex-husband even after she found his hell-raising ways too much to bear, even after she divorced him and remarried, knows how many of Jack's tales have any basis in fact, and possibly she doesn't know either. Jack certainly forgot long ago.

In contrast, Dylan's fantasies were rather less complex, though he did tend to overplay the borrowed 'Woody's old buddy' image, to which he had even less right than Elliott. In an age of alienated youth and generation gap politics he also assumed an estrangement from his family which fitted the fantasies of audience rather better than the carefully concealed truth: that Bobby was a good Jewish son who started sending money home as soon as he started to make it, and still does.

Someone with rather more *chutzpah* than me ought to make a study of how much of the folk cowboy fantasy that lies at the heart of American rock and roll is a simple reaction against the Jewish culture of their childhood.

After all, when one considers the mass genocide which was the true history of white America's colonial wars against the indigenous population, the cowboy image is a remarkable fantasy for the rebellious young of the new electronic culture to espouse: it is rather as if the rebels of a future age were to take to wearing green berets and pinning up Lt Calley posters in the places of honour now occupied by Che in their crash pads. Though when one considers the appeal that the detritus of the Nazi comic-book horror has for the Hells Angels, perhaps our ability to turn any symbol to the direction we choose is no more surprising than the fact that the tune of the 'Horst Wessel Lied' was once a Communist hymn, and the swastika was the fire sign of the great Norse god Thor, the sun's sign of life until the Nazis threw it into reverse.

Rumour has it that Bob is now an undercover Zionist and is planning to change his name back to Zimmerman at the next opportunity. He spent much of the summer of 1971 in Israel, though one night when he stayed at the same hotel as actor Nicol Williamson he was forced to move out to another hotel so he could get some sleep: Williamson's bawdy songs were keeping him awake.

There was a time when people used to complain about the noise Dylan's party made in hotels when he was on tour. There's that beautiful scene in D. A. Pennebaker's not very inspiring cinema verité film about Dylan, 'Don't Look Back', in which Dylan's manager, Al Grossman, delivers exactly the sort of *coup de grâce* we've all wanted to lay on a sassy flunky in one of those hotels: 'There's been no noise in this room, and you're one of the dumbest assholes and the most stupid persons I've ever spoken to in my life. If we were some place else I'd punch you in your goddam nose, you stupid nut. Would you ... we've rented this room and I'm asking you to leave this room. We have valuables in here and I don't want you in here.'

Later in the same movie, Dylan himself reproves a drunk who drops a glass out of his hotel-room window: 'If you know who did it you just better tell whoever did it to get out there and tell the cats that come up here to ask who did it, tell them who it was. I'm not taking no fucking responsibility for cats I don't know, man. I got enough responsibility with my own friends and my own people.'

Things have changed.

That was the last acoustic tour, 1965, and Bobbie was still thought of as in the folk bag, though he told the *Time* magazine interviewer, in the film, that he wasn't '... and I don't think I'm a folk singer. You'll probably call me a folk singer but, you know, the other people know better because the people, you know, that buy my records, listen to me, don't necessarily read *Time* magazine.'

Later that same year Bobbie took his electric friends to Forest Hills and to the Newport Folk Festival and got himself booed by the homespun liberals who refused to understand, who didn't want to understand, who sensed instinctively that rock was a working class music, a black music (the first electric guitar in pop was played by a black man, T-Bone Walker) and what was even worse, an urban music. This was tougher to handle than the decrepit traditions of the Appalachians.

It was not, however, the very first time he had been booed. That had happened in December of 1963, two short months after the Cuban missile crisis had inspired Dylan to compose his most apocalyptic song, 'A Hard Rain's Gonna Fall', which with its mixture of nursery rhyme question-and-answer and William Blake surrealist imagery summed up the near-disaster that Kennedy and Khrushchev almost brought the world to, between them. In the interim, also Kennedy had been killed, some said by a lone madman, others by a monstrous conspiracy, and the only thing that made the former easier to believe than the latter was the knowledge that Kennedy was much less of a danger to the military-industrial complex ruling America than had been Roosevelt in the days of New Deal. On the other hand, the evidence surely pointed to one thing: the official story had more holes shot in it than Kennedy had in his head.

Then a left wing body called the Emergency Civil Liberties Committee decided to give Bob Dylan their Tom Paine award. Bob had been singing for SNCC in the south, down where heads were liable to get busted, but there in the Grand Ballroom of the Americana Hotel he came up against a different kind of left-winger, the kind who wear evening dress and pearls, or a tuxedo and black tie. It was something of a shock, the way he told it in an interview with Nat Hentoff in the *New Yorker* the following year: 'As soon as I got there, I felt uptight. First of all, the people with me couldn't get in. They looked even funkier than I did, I guess. They weren't dressed right, or something.

'Inside the ballroom, I really got uptight. I began to drink. I looked down from the platform and saw a bunch of people who had nothing to do with my kind of politics.

I looked down and I got scared. They were supposed to be on my side, but I didn't feel any connection with them. Here were these people who'd been all involved with the left in the Thirties, and now they were supporting Civil Rights drives. That's groovy, but they also had minks and jewels, and it was like they were giving the money out of guilt.

'I got up to leave, and they followed me and caught me. They told me I had to accept the award. When I got up to make my speech, I couldn't say anything by that time but what was passing through my mind.

'They'd been talking about Kennedy being killed, and Bill Moore and Medgar Evers and the Buddhist monks in Vietnam being killed. I had to say something about Lee Oswald. I told them I'd read a lot of his feelings in the papers, and I knew he was uptight. Said I'd been uptight, too, so I'd got a lot of his feelings. I saw a lot of myself in Oswald, I said, and I saw in him a lot of the times we're all living in.

'And, you know, they started booing. They looked at me like I was an animal. They actually thought I was saying it was a good thing Kennedy had been killed. That's how far out they are. I was talking about Oswald.

'And then I started talking about friends of mine in Harlem – some of them junkies, all of them poor. And I said they need freedom as much as anybody else, and what's anybody doing for *them*?

'The chairman was kicking my leg under the table, and I told him, "Get out of here".

'Now, what I was supposed to be was a nice cat. I was supposed to say, "I appreciate your award and I'm a great singer and I'm a great believer in liberals, and you buy my records and I'll support your cause". But I didn't, and so I wasn't accepted that night....

'...You know, they were talking about Freedom Fighters that night. I've been in Mississippi, man. I know those people on another level besides Civil Rights cam-

paigns. I know them as friends. Like Jim Forman, one of
the heads of SNCC. I'll stand on his side any time. But
those people that night were actually getting me to look
at coloured people as coloured people.

'I tell you, I'm never going to have anything to do with
any political organization again in my life. Oh, I might
help a friend if he was campaigning for office. But I'm not
going to be part of any organization.

'Those people at that dinner were the same as everybody else. They're doing their time. They're chained to
what they're doing. The only thing is, they're trying to
put morals and great deeds on their chains, but basically
they don't want to jeopardize their positions. They got
their jobs to keep. There's nothing there for me, and
there's nothing there for the kind of people I hang around
with.

'The only thing I'm sorry about is I guess I hurt the
collection at the dinner. I didn't know they were going to
try to collect money after my speech. I guess I lost them a
lot of money. Well, I offered to pay them whatever it
was they figured they'd lost because of the way I talked.
I told them I didn't care how much it was. I hate debts,
especially moral debts. They're worse than money debts.'

The Marxist mafia! The people who plan the revolution,
who will run the new society after it has happened, are
already quite high in the echelons of those running the old
society. What they are arguing about basically is who runs
the machine, who's going to be top of the heap. None of
them think for a moment that the machine might not be
worth running.

The toughest capitalist I know, the trickiest to deal with
(I have negotiated contracts with him) also spends much
of his spare time organizing events like that, raising funds
for the British Communist Party. I've been to his factory;
it's no model of the new society showing us all how it
ought to be done, and I know if I bothered to tax him
with this, he'd have convincing and well-argued Marxist

reasons to explain why piecemeal reforms will, if anything, only help to strengthen the system he hopes one day to see replaced. By what? Who will be managing director of his factory then? Try and guess.

The effect of the Americana dinner upon Dylan's future development was decisive, and it is impossible to understand what he has done subsequently if you know nothing about it, and yet you will search in vain through most of the popular left press of the following months for any report of it. *Sing Out!* magazine, which with *Broadside* had been Dylan's most consistent advocate, carried no report of the dinner, though later in 1964 Irwin Silber wrote an insulting, patronizing open letter to the boy he'd lionized only a twelvemonth or so before: 'You seem to be a different kind of boy now, Bob – and I'm worried about it. I saw at Newport how you had somehow lost contact with people. It seemed to me that some of the paraphernalia of fame were getting in your way.

'You travel with an entourage now – with good buddies who are going to laugh when you need laughing and drink wine with you and insure your privacy – and never challenge you to face everyone else's reality again.'

Having come up against the entourage and had them hustle me so fast out of his privacy, I can see the truth at the heart of what Silber was saying, because what he was really complaining about was being hustled out, too.

Like all the folkie-Marxist critics of the 'another side' that had emerged at that recording session when Nat Hentoff interviewed him for the *New Yorker* profile, Silber accused Dylan of chickening out from the real world in his later lyrics: 'Your new songs seem to be all inner-directed now, inner-probing, self-conscious – maybe even a little maudlin or a little cruel on occasion.'

A slightly more perceptive critic, though with a roughly similar standpoint, Josh Dunson, said much the same thing in his rather sketchy panorama of protest songwriting, 'Freedom in the Air', in 1965: 'In the current stage of his song writing, there seems to be an attempt to try and recapture some of the humour and personal statement typical of his early writings. There is also the explicit rejection of outright political statement. His latest album, "Another Side of Bob Dylan", recorded in one session, contains a minimum of political statement and includes a composition which relegates his early more political songs to a time when he was "older". On this record, Bob claims he is "younger now" and therefore writing songs that offer no moral judgements.'

The phrase '*I was so much older then, I'm younger than that now*' is of a piece with his farewell to the Marxist-liberal establishment, 'Positively Fourth Street'.

The following year, Dunson was to make a fatuous comparison which almost closes the discussion here and now upon a completely derisory note: 'Listen to Dylan's "Fourth Street" side by side with a "race" record that made the white charts like Ramsey Lewis Trio's "The In Crowd" and one is water and the other is gin.'

Presumably by that comparison he is trying to say that the cocktail lounge 'soul' of Ramsey Lewis's derivative, unimaginative, plodding piano has more guts to it than a song which has the courage to buck the whole leftist power structure of pop and tell us exactly which way he is heading. It wasn't the absence of political commitment that upset them, but the fact that his commitment was leading him to criticize the politicos themselves.

The songs on 'Another Side of Bob Dylan' *are* more personal than those that went before. That is the great part of their strength. But these critics were wrong in their contention that the inner and outer worlds were mutually exclusive, that to care about the world one must diminish oneself, that to care about oneself is to reject the needs of others. This is but the same old flesh-or-the-spirit dichotomy which is the dubious heritage of the Judaeo-Christian tradition, and which at its most schizophrenic is the typical pathology of our time.

R. D. Laing has pointed out that alienation from self creates the schizophrenic 'unembodied' person: 'The embodied person has a sense of being flesh and blood and bones, of being biologically alive and real; he knows himself to be substantial. To the extent that he is thoroughly "in" his body, he is likely to have a sense of personal continuity in time. He will experience himself as subject to the dangers that threaten his body, the dangers of attack, mutilation, disease, decay and death. He is implicated in bodily desire, and the gratifications and frustrations of the body. The individual thus has as his starting-point an experience of his body as a base from which he can be a person with other human beings. . . .

'. . . a divorce of self from body deprives the unembodied self from direct participation in the life of the world, which is mediated exclusively through the body's perceptions, feelings, and movements (expressions, gestures, words, actions, etc). The unembodied self, as an onlooker at all the body does, engages in nothing directly. Its functions come to be observation, control, and criticism vis-à-vis what the body is experiencing and doing, and those operations which are usually spoken of as purely "mental".' Marxist materialism, indeed, has much of its philosophical foundations in Pythagorean mysticism.

The other performers were more understanding of the way Dylan was changing than the critics. A much more consistently political songwriter than Dylan had ever been (though unfortunately also his technical inferior), Phil Ochs was saying at the same time: 'I'm quite sure Dylan despises what I write. I've talked to him about this at some length – and I get the impression he can't accept what I'm doing. Because in his mind it's political and therefore bullshit. Because I'm not writing about myself and my deepest emotions, he feels. And I'm not facing the thing as brutally honestly as he is – in other words, he thinks that I could be much more honest with myself. And this is the disturbing thing. Here's the man I most respect in the world, Dylan, telling me that.... And I have to search myself all the time, ask myself what am I doing, am I kidding myself, is Dylan kidding himself about politics, and the more I think about it the more I'm convinced we're both valid.... And I keep coming up with the answer that I think I am doing the right thing. I think Dylan makes a basic mistake in rejecting his old writing and my writing....

'... I really hope he doesn't become too violent in putting down his former self, because, in the end, I think, that will limit him as a writer. He will limit his scope. I still maintain he could have gone much further than he did in the idiom of social realism. And even now he can go back and do it. I think that's what he did, essentially, when he wrote "It's Alright Ma". In it he combined the old Dylan and the new and it's one of his very best songs because it brought together the best elements of the two ...' (*Broadside* magazine, October 15, 1965).

The problem of a singer's past compositions haunts many of the new writers. In 1968 Jim Morrison was writing:

'The old get old and the young get stronger.
Might take a week or it might take longer.
They've got the guns, love, we've got the numbers.
Going to win, yeah, we're taking over.'
Come on!'

I asked him a while later how he felt about the song after the police riot on the streets of Chicago during the Democratic Convention, when the battle had gone, decidedly to the cops. I asked him how he felt, remembering that, when he sang those confident words about taking over, on stage now.

'It's a song, man,' he said. 'It's how I felt when I wrote it. That's its validity. Now it's just a song. Chicago didn't change my memory of how I felt when I wrote the song.'

As a matter of record, Dylan hasn't really rejected his earlier songs, though he admitted to Nat Hentoff that some of them were written because he knew they would go down well with the liberals: 'Those records I've already made, I'll stand behind them, but some of that was jumping on the scene to be heard and a lot of it was because I didn't see anybody else doing that kind of thing.'

Actually, 'Another Side' contains songs which distinctly broaden the range of Dylan's compassion. 'Chimes of Freedom', for instance, a remarkable vision encapsulated within the dramatic portrayal of a thunderstorm, extends its sympathy to the rebel (placed, significantly perhaps, first) but also to the prostitute, the homosexual, and ultimately to *'every hung-up person in the whole wide universe'*.

It is significant that the song is called 'Chimes of Freedom', for Dylan was at the time evolving an existential attitude towards freedom that was being defined in his songs: 'What's wrong is how few people are free. Most people walking around are tied down to something that doesn't let them really *speak*, so they just add their confusion to the mess. I mean, they have some kind of vested interest in the way things are now.' (In the context of what he was saying, still referring to the liberals he'd met at the Americana Hotel, that is a very perceptive remark: it wasn't until May 1968 that one of the largest Communist Parties in the capitalist world, the French, was to illustrate dramatically how strongly it identified itself with the status quo.)

'. . . All I can do is show the people who ask me questions how I live. All I can do is be me.'

(*'Yoko and me. And that's reality.'*)

'I can't tell them how to change things, because there's only one way to change things, and that's to cut yourself off from all the chains. That's hard for most people to do. . . .'

'I can't think for you, you have to decide.' It was not a new thought of Dylan's. *Sing Out!* had put it on their front page in December 1963. And though 'Another Side'

and what followed marked a qualitative change in his development, it was not such a radical break with the past as everyone then assumed.

And the electric sound of Forest Hills and Newport, 1965, shouldn't have been the shock it was, for that, too, had been foreshadowed already. On 'Another Side', the phantasmagoric 'Motorpsycho Nightmare' not merely highlights the confrontation between the hip urban hobo and the reactionary rural redneck which was a feature of 'Easy Rider'; it also marks Dylan's return to his real roots, to the black rhythm and blues he used to listen to on the radio as a kid, the music of Chuck Berry. The tune is recognizably related to Berry's 'Johnny B. Goode', the first of a veritable saga of Chuck Berry songs about a hip young black who uses his guitar as a key to success, a pattern which was to be copied by many white boys after and including Dylan. Not so many black boys made it in real life, however, not even Chuck Berry.

After 'Motorpsycho Nightmare', which upset Josh Dunson because of its frank acknowledgement of the gap between town and country life styles and attitudes, 'Subterranean Homesick Blues' shouldn't have caught them unprepared, for all that happened was he plugged in the guitar and added Robbie Robertson, the young Canadian guitar genius who'd wailed so effectively on Ronnie Hawkins' revival of the Bo Diddley hit, 'Who Do You Love?'. The tune was again related to a black original, and this time not only the melodic root but also the very syntax of the poetry from the Chuck Berry number, 'Too Much Monkey Business', was utilized to portray so vividly the piled-on persecutions of a hostile environment.

Berry's song is a graphic description of the life of the urban black in a series of cameo-like verses, and it is typical of the blinkered lives of most white liberals that they only heard the song *after* they had started to try to understand 'Subterranean Homesick Blues'. But the kids, black and white, got the reference, and straight away dug

the parallels Dylan was drawing between two existences.
Chuck Berry:
'Runnin' to an' fro, hard workin' at the mill,
Never fail in the mail it come a rotten bill.

'Too much monkey business,
Too much monkey business,
Too much monkey business
For me to be involved in.

'Salesman talkin' to me tryin' to run me up a creek:
You can buy it, go an' try it, you can pay me next
    week – ah!

'. . . I don't want your botheration,
Get away, leave me.
'Too much monkey business for you
Too much monkey business for me.'

As Charlie Gillett has pointed out, Chuck Berry's songs,
'performed in a blues style and presenting in their themes
some strong criticisms of aspects of American life' were
ignored by showbiz, though his country rock debut disc,
the less unusual 'Maybellene', hit the top ten in 1955.

'Judges and courts in "Thirty Days", credit and car
salesmen in "No Money Down", high culture in "Roll
Over Beethoven", and all these plus more in "Too Much
Monkey Business" were cause for complaint. Since these
records were performed in a strong "blues" voice, the
songs, with the exception of "Roll Over Beethoven", which
had a brilliant rolling rhythm and a lyric that was particular
to adolescents rather than a general one oriented to
adults (as were the others), received relatively little attention from the disc jockeys.'

Berry had also pioneered a lyrical recognition of the
alienation of the young (and especially, in his case, the
alienation of the *black* young, of course) which was a long
way closer to reality than the crew-cut Andy Hardy cute-
ness of the conventional 'schooldays' genre of songs by

Buddy Holly. Berry thus led the way directly towards 'Subterranean Homesick Blues', a song which is a brilliant sequence of aphorisms crammed tigher into the lyric than Solomon's proverbs are packed into the Bible, with the same sort of concrete reality that distinguished Chuck Berry's best lyrics, giving advice on how to survive in the urban jungle, the dangers of trusting the police, the accelerating breakdown of industrial society. The first one-and-a half verses were the first recognition in a white song-writer's work of the part that marijuana was playing in this new sub-culture.

I have often taken the words at the end of the third verse – '*Don't follow leaders, Watch the parkin' meters*' – as the embodiment of where we are today, for if you count the growth of parking meters you really have a simple statistical index of the decay of the communications system of the industrial state, while '*Don't follow leaders*' could well be the keynote text for this entire book.

Far from cutting Dylan off from the political mainstream, this song brought him back to the centre of things in a rather remarkable way, for the extreme left wing terrorists in America calling themselves the Weathermen got their name from one of the song's statements:

You don't need a weatherman
To know which way the wind blows.'

However, unless they gave themselves the name with some profound, satirical intent, one can only assume that, like so many leftists, they have not been paying careful enough attention, ignoring the obvious intent of the text to make it mean what they wish it to. After all, it does say '*You* don't *need a weatherman*', and in fact the point the song is making is precisely that, that the elitist presumption of a middle-class intellectual like Regis Debray, who seeks to politicize the oppressed and show them the approved way out of their plight, is not merely what we don't need, but it's counter-productive.

'Another Side of Bob Dylan' and his subsequent work

were specific rejections of this prophetic role: 'Now a lot
of people are doing finger-pointing songs. You know –
pointing to all the things that are wrong. Me, I don't want
to write *for* people any more. You know – be a spokesman.
Like I once wrote about Emmett Till in the first person,
pretending I was him. From now on, I want to write from
inside me, and to do that I'm going to have to get back
to writing like I used to when I was ten – having everything come out naturally. The way I like to write is for it
to come out the way I walk or talk. . . .'

As Matisse says, it takes great skill to learn to paint
like a child. Which is one of the meanings of *'But I was
so much older then, I'm younger than that now'*.

The thing the compulsive folkies failed to recognize was
that in this new, 'uncommitted' posture, Dylan was moving
closer to the position of the self-effacing folk bard:

> *'My name is nothing extry*
> *So that I will not tell.'*

As E. S. Carpenter said of the Eskimo bards: 'In oral
tradition, the myth-teller speaks as many-to-many, not as
person-to-person. Speech and song are addressed to all.'
They were so hung-up on Dylan's instrumentation, thinking
simply that acoustic guitar equals folk and electric guitar
equals pop, thus betraying the basic racism which their
ignorance of a great folk poet like Chuck Berry also indi-
cates, for unless one excluded black musicians, one has to
accept the fact that the electric guitar is actually the most
widely-spread folk instrument in the English-speaking
world.

More, since the highly vocalized, singing notes of the
electric instrument direct the player towards melody rather
than the harmonies which spring from the chorded
acoustic guitar, the electric instrument is academically *more*
appropriate to folk music, in terms of its basic function,
than the acoustic guitar, being dionysian in inspiration, kin
to the twin aulos of ancient Marsyas, while the acoustic

K

guitar is heir to the apollonian tradition of literate, educated man. In their hostility to electric rock, the Marxist folkies of the Sixties were telling us more of their origins than they knew, for the victory of eye over ear which is told in myth as the triumph of cultivated Apollo over rough, uncouth Marsyas, is now being reversed, and we return to the oral society of the transistor radio, the long-play stereo record, the comic book, and the TV cassette. Meanwhile, the critics fight a rearguard action by elevating rock and roll to the level of high art, leading many of its practitioners into the elitist blind alley labelled 'progressive' or 'underground'.

The literate critics complained that they could not understand the words Dylan was singing on 'Subterranean Homesick Blues' though actually his diction was clearer than ever. It was possibly the collage effect, the rapid juxtaposition of one apparently unrelated image after another that baffled their minds, used to the linear progressions of Euclidean logic rather than the multi-dimensional mosaic inter-relationships which have been revealed by Einstein to be a more valid image of the entropy which surrounds man.

However, this contention that Dylan's words are deliberately obscure is not restricted to his critics. There is a young American Dylan fan called Alan J. Weberman who has developed what he says is the 'secret language' that Dylan has devised to get his message across to his devotees, and he goes to extreme lengths, even sifting through the garbage of Dylan's New York home for clues in the form of scraps of abandoned work or thrown-away letters that may help him to justify his thesis. His heart is so in the old message-delivering Dylan of the mid-Sixties that he even dresses like Dylan did then, in the hat he wore on the cover of his first record, and which John Lennon also wore on the cover of 'In His Own Write'. He maintains he has learned from the 'secret language' of Dylan's newest songs that he is currently the victim of a heroin habit, and is trying to get the people to anaesthetize themselves similarly to avoid the necessity for social change. Dylan treated these 'analyses' of his work at first with amusement, but then as time went on and Weberman insisted he was a junkie even in the absence of any telltale track marks that would be left on Dylan's arms by the needles, he became more and more irritated. So at the same time Weberman's attitude hardened in reaction.

At first, however, he was fairly charitable. 'Dylan was trying to get a political message on to AM radio,' was an earlier explanation. 'The only way he could do this was to make his ideas as cryptic as possible. His language had to be something that straights wouldn't respond to – but that the kids would find. I knew that Dylan had put the meanings there for people like me to find. So I decided to dedicate myself to explaining the secret language of rock to the world.'

Dylan isn't the only rock artist using this secret language, thinks Weberman, and he explains that Creedence Clearwater Revival's 'Wish I Could Hide Away' is a private message to Dylan telling him to abandon his heroin and get ready for revolution.

This is a game that not only Weberman plays, though when he does it his neurosis shows rather more plainly than with other, more respectable and accepted critics. They had a field day with the songs on 'Sgt Pepper', spotting with glee that the initials of 'Lucy in the Sky With Diamonds' spelt LSD and so on. I believe Lennon when he says it isn't so. It's not as if he denies the other drug references on the album – *'I'd love to turn you on'* – so at least when he denies the significance of the initials we might as well believe him, even though it is kind of a weird coincidence, that particular song being such an obvious acid trip.

Using similar techniques to Weberman's, and following in the footsteps of those critics who seek a concrete interpretation of every image, like as if they were a secret code

addressed to themselves alone, I have proved to my
own satisfaction that 'For the Benefit of Mr Kite' on
'Pepper' is actually about the Cuban missiles crisis. I'm
joking, of course, and it's well-known that Lennon cribbed
much of the song from an old circus poster he saw, but
the joy of this kind of interpretation is that once you have
thought of it, even as fantasy, you are constantly running
across new parallel meanings which back up the interpretation, even if you didn't start out serious.

'*For the benefit of Mr Kite,*' goes the song, describing
him later as '*The celebrated Mr K*', an abbreviation our
headline-seeking press created for Khrushchev. As Bertrand Russell said, it was Khrushchev who really called
the tune over Cuba. 'I asked myself if there were no sane
men in the seats of power. At the last possible moment,
the answer came: Yes, there was one sane man. It happened that he was on the side of Russia. This was an
unimportant accident. His sanity saved the world.'

Or as John Lennon puts its:

'*Lastly through a hogshead of real fire!*
In this way Mr K will challenge the world!'

'*The Hendersons will all be there*' – John F. and Robert
F. and Edward, only their real name's Kennedy. '*Late of
Pablo Fanques Fair*' is the Bay of Pigs invasion by the
Cuban emigres. '*And of course Henry the Horse dances
the waltz*' is a reference to Lyndon B. Johnson, then the
rootin' tootin' shootin' vice-president.

'*The band begins at ten to six*
Mr K performs his tricks
Without a sound.'

In other words, the way he sneaked the missiles into Cuba
without being spotted until he had them on their launching
sites. On the other hand, Kennedy felt he was in a stronger
position to take risks than Khrushchev:

'*And Mr H will demonstrate*
Ten summersets he'll undertake
On solid ground.'

But (and this is the whole point of the song) the event is a monstrous put-up job by Kennedy and Khrushchev to bamboozle us:

'Messrs K and H assure the public
Their production will be second to none.'

And so on.

Of course, it's a load of crap, and so are most of Weberman's interpretations of Dylan. Sometimes he stumbles upon some different levels of meaning. It is fairly obvious that the 'parting' songs on 'Another Side' can be read as more than bitter-sweet lovesongs, that 'It Ain't Me Babe' has more than a hint of a refusal in it to play the part demanded by the leftists any more:

'... someone
Who will promise never to part
Someone to close his eyes for you
Someone to close his heart
Someone to die for you an' more....'

but this is so clear that it doesn't need any key to the secret language to help us decipher the other layer of meaning. And it doesn't mean that it isn't *also* just a simple lovesong.

You could write off Weberman as just another crank, were it not that, like Dylan (Zimmerman), he is a Jew, for as George Steiner has shown, the part that Jewish concern with words for their own sake has played in the formation of Western literate culture is considerable. This concern prevented Freud's techniques of psychoanalysis from being capable of development beyond the point to which he took them, and indeed make the practice of psycho-analysis virtually unworkable when dealing with the illiterate.

The stumbling blocks which trip the analyst in such cases, says Steiner, are literary. 'Psycho-analysis is a *matter of words* – words heard, glossed, stumbled over, exchanged ... only the educated, leisured classes of society exhibit the degree of verbalization, of multiple semantic reference, of decorous elision, indispensable to the analytic process.'

This reliance on literary forms extends to the very technical terms used by psychiatrists, as Laing says: 'How can I go straight to my patients if the psychiatric words at my disposal keep the patient at a distance from me? How can one demonstrate the general human relevance and significance of the patient's condition if the words one has to use are specifically designed to isolate and circumscribe the meaning of the patient's life to a particular clinical entity? . . .

'The words of the current technical vocabulary either refer to man in isolation from the other and the world, that is, as an entity not *essentially* "in relation to" the other and in a world, or they refer to falsely substantialized aspects of this isolated entity. Such words are: mind and body, psyche and soma, psychological and physical, personality, the self, the organism . . .' (The Divided Self).

Steiner shows how Freud tried to use the word as a brain-washing tool; but it only worked on the literate, and then it could not cure, only reveal what was wrong. For, as Steiner shows, the psychic trauma charted by Freud so vividly had its roots in the social trauma in which the machine of society was literally shaking itself apart: 'Today, psycho-analysis looks more and more like an inspired construct of the historical and poetic imagination, like one of those dynamic fictions through which the master-builders of the Nineteenth Century – Hegel, Balzac, Auguste Comte – summarized and gave communicative force to their highly personal, dramatic readings of man and society . . . the work of Freud impresses one as a superbly perceptive, eloquent summation, already tinged with a stoic premonition of the incipient ruin, of European bourgeois humanism, floruit 1789 – 1914. Freud's mapping – dare one say mythology – of human motives and behaviour is profoundly circumstantial. It mirrors, it codifies rationally the economic and social assumptions, the erotic mores, the domestic rites of the Central European urban middle class in the years from 1880 to the collapse of agreed values in the first World War....

'...the "locality" and profoundly literary quality of Freud's unravelling ... are firmly bound to the expressive and suppressive idiom of the Central European, largely Jewish middle class of the late Nineteenth Century in which Freud himself came of age. Freud's descriptions of the actions of consciousness and of the unconscious cannot be dissociated from the grammatical structures and referential conventions (referential especially in regard to slang and to literature) of German and Austrian German in the age of von Hofmannsthal, Arthur Schnitzler, and Thomas Mann.'

How much of the Judaism ingested by Western European culture when it made Christianity the established religion has now become part of the very fabric of the state? One has only to re-read the Gospels to see how much of early Christianity, despite its assumption of the Messianic mantle, was a struggle against the extreme literary bias of the Scribes and Pharisees, adhering to the letter of the Law: 'The Sabbath was made for man, and not man for the Sabbath' (Mark ii, 27) ... 'Therefore all things whatsoever ye would that men should do to you, do ye even so to them: for *this* is the Law and the prophets' (Matthew vii, 12) ... 'Man shall not live by bread alone, but by every word that proceedeth out of the mouth of God' (Matthew iv, 4) – the spoken word over the written Law.

Thus the original doctrine of Christianity, as passed down, orally, by word-of-mouth by the persecuted followers of the martyred at springtime, half-mythical Christ, who held all things in common, whose band of 12 disciples plus one was taken as a model (or was it an analogue?) by the witch covens formed 1,400 years later in resistance to the persecutions of the age of print.

After the rule of Paul, all was different: 'And the tongue is a fire, a world of iniquity: so is the tongue among our members, that it defileth the whole body, and setteth on

fire the course of nature; and it is set on fire of hell.'
Thus the fire-eating disciple James, in his 'General Epistle',
five brief chapters of fire and brimstone. His distrust of the
spoken word harks back, perhaps, to the Judaic proverb:
'An ungodly man diggeth up evil: and in his lips there is
as a burning fire.' (Proverbs xiv, 27) rather than to the
chiding by the Christ of those who 'do worship me,
teaching for doctrines the commandments of men'. It was
in this context that Christ said: 'Not that which goeth
into the mouth defileth a man; but that which cometh out
of the mouth, this defileth a man' (Matthew xv, 11). The
fact that the Pharisees 'were offended, after they heard
this saying' is its own explanation.

Steiner himself sees the central role of the literary heirs
of the Pharisees in expressing the particular crisis now
coming to its conclusion: '. . . In these philosophers, poets
and critics was manifest the realization, crystallized by the
catastrophe of world war, that humanism, as it had ener-
gized European consciousness since the Renaissance, was
in a process of collapse . . . (The dominant role of Jews
in this movement of terror and genius would be worth
assessing. Did the Jew have an especial affinity to the life
of language, the written word having been, for so long,
his primary homeland?)'

Turning his back on demands for him to define his words
in literally understandable terms is not the only way in
which Dylan escapes from his Judaic background, whether
he calls himself Zimmerman or Dylan. There is also his
refusal of the Messianic mantle. The part that a liberator-
to-come must play in human progress is one of the central
themes of Marxist orthodoxies, and they differ from earlier
worshippers of the heroic individual only in seeing such
giants as the creations of the historical process rather than
of Jehovah or even of their own will. And yet the historical
process, by which human culture is developed in ways
largely outside the direct control of human beings, is very
like another, less personal Jehovah, is it not?

Dylan very much does not wish to be a Messiah, an example to be followed by the rest of his generation. Nothing worries him more. 'I am by no means an example for any kid wanting to strike out. I mean, I wouldn't want a young kid to leave home because I did it, and then have to go through a lot of the things I went through. Everybody has to find his *own* way to be free. There isn't anybody who can help you in that sense . . .' he told Hentoff.

When he delved back into his roots in 'Bringing It All Back Home' (the title of the album was significant), it was something he was doing for himself. His shock at the booing was only too evident: the philistines at Newport had him in tears. What was less well publicised was his reaction to the effect that his move had on the then flourishing American folk revival scene, inducing hundreds to throw away their acoustic Gibsons and Martins and form themselves into rock and roll bands. The result was very healthy for rock, for most of the best of the intellectual rockers of the Sixties, people like Joe McDonald and Grace Slick and John Sebastian and John Phillips, were ex-folkies. They brought something strong out of folk into their music.

Nevertheless, what worried Dylan was the thought that he had, despite himself, become an example once again. Or so it seemed. He confessed a deep disturbance at the phenomenon to Louis Killen, the English traditionalist singer on tour of America, when he dropped into Killen's Woodstock concert incognito during the period of his withdrawal, after the motorcycle accident which changed him so basically, altering even the timbre of his voice.

Again he tried to change the pattern, moving away from rock into the area of white country music which had been the basis of early rock and roll, music which was closer to the folk influences that had affected him in New York, and thus superficially similar. This allowed the folk critics to tell themselves that the old Dylan was returning to them again, and they were encouraged in the thought by the fact that he recorded 'Girl from the North Country', one of his old songs. But he was doing nothing of the sort.

The songs on 'John Wesley Harding' were allusive, deceptively simple, often ironic, so spare in their use of words in contrast with the great 17-minute gushes that had filled one whole side of 'Blonde on Blonde' with just one song, that the listener had to work hard to fill in the details of what was going on himself.

He explained the difference between what he was doing and folk techniques in an interview in *Sing Out!* in 1968: 'See, on the album, you have to think about it after you hear it, that's what takes up the time, but with a ballad, you don't necessarily have to think about it after you hear it, it can all unfold to you. These melodies on the "John Wesley Harding" album lack this traditional sense of time. As with the third verse of "The Wicked Messenger", which opens it up, and then the time schedule takes a jump and soon the time becomes wider. One realizes that when one hears it, but one might adapt to it. But we are not hearing anything that isn't there; anything we can imagine is really there. The same thing is true of the song "All Along the Watchtower" which opens up in a slightly different way, in a stranger way, for here we have the cycle of events working in a rather reverse order.'

Even the title song indicated that not all was what it seemed, for John Wesley Harding (more correctly: Hardin) was not at all the gallant Robin Hood figure described in the son, as anyone who knew enough about him to want to write a song about him would know. Of course, Jesse James wasn't at all the 'friend to the poor' the ballads paint, either, and possibly in 'John Wesley Harding' Dylan was saying something about myths, being something of a myth himself. The difference being that the Jesse James legends accumulated over a period of years, while Dylan's song seems to be attempting to falsify the record of the life of a racist thug at one stroke. He must have known this would fail, so we are forced to ask ourselves again what he was about. No, there was nothing simple about this record.

The musicians on the record were Nashville session men, highly paid professional musicians who'd work, like mercenaries selling their swords, for any artist who came to the studios. By going down to the heart of Tennessee for his come-back album, Dylan was beginning an entente with country music, derogated by intellectual hippies as 'shit-kicking music', that was to continue throughout the next three or four albums.

The significant difference with previous changes of direction was that here Dylan wasn't leading any movement: he was becoming part of something that was already happening. As a matter of fact, he didn't really lead the folkies into the electric land of rock and roll either, for it was a natural progression; however, the defection of such a weighty folk name probably hurried the process on.

In his move towards country music, Dylan was following rather than leading, for a number of his old friends were already into country sounds: Roger McGuinn of the Byrds, ex-Byrds Gram Parsons and Chris Hillman who formed a rock band that had a classic country band line-up, including the wailing pedal steel guitar that had been developed by Nashville technology out of the original acoustic dobro, which had brought singing melody to the guitar even before electrification.

At the same time, folk bands like the Dillards bluegrass group were moving towards the Nashville sound, and Doug Dillard left to join Gene Clark, another ex-Byrd, to form another country-styled rock band.

Simultaneously, Robbie Robertson and the other Canadian boys who had got their share of the booing when Dylan toured Europe, known as the Hawks when they played with Ronnie Hawkins, as the Crackers with Dylan, and now calling themselves simply the Band, were taking rock back to the sort of elemental themes that were the natural currency of folk music.

This was perhaps the most important thing that was happening, for the musical accommodation could be merely a formal adoption of country trappings, the pedal steel and the rest, the high-toned vocal style of singing which, traced back through the bluegrass of Bill Monroe and the high, lonesome sound of Roscoe Holcomb had its origin in mountain gospel singing, and the strange blend of concrete reality and wishful thinking fantasy that is the subject of so many Nashville lyrics. What was more important was the recognition of the country community's alternative lifestyle as something just as valid – and just as threatened by the disintegrating American industrial state – as that of the urban hip.

In political terms, the realization was spreading that any revolution which didn't take into account the feelings, traditions and even the prejudices of the working class population, and especially the non-industrialized white working class of the rural south, would merely be throwing them into the arms of the extreme right. Till then, the most that had been achieved was to recognize the existence of a gap between town and country, as Dylan had done in 'Motorpsycho Nightmare' and which, rather late in the day and quite unconstructively, the movie 'Easy Rider' did also. While the urban kids were trying to construct for themselves communities as viable alternatives to the soulless industrial state–failing most times – the white southerners had a sense of community tradition that was not yet completely destroyed, however much decay and the exploitation from the industrial north had weakened it, turning its forms in upon itself, and however much right-wing opportunists like Wallace and the Klan might use racist and reactionary delusions to pervert the community purpose and turn it against potential allies like black militants and hippie transients in particular.

It was for this reason that Dylan chose not to sing his own songs for the soundtrack of 'Easy Rider', because he felt that the conclusion of the movie was too negative, that no satisfactory solution had been found to the communications problem posed so clearly by the confrontation between the two motorcyclist heroes and the rigid, over-formalized community traditions of the lands through which they travelled. It's interesting, by the way, that he wasn't insisting upon any over-easy peace-and-love reconciliation between the two counterposed ways of life. On the contrary, rather than Peter Fonda being killed as well as Dennis Hopper (a scene which has raised cheers when the film has been shown in Southern movie houses), he wanted Fonda to even up the score somehow.

And so the significance of Dylan's most recent direction is doubly important: first, he is very much a rank-and-file member of a musical movement that he did not himself instigate, and he is showing no sign of taking over its leadership as he did, whether he liked it or not, with the American folk revival in the early Sixties. But also he is digging deep inside himself, right back to his true roots, avoiding the easy, safe, processed and pre-packaged view of a virtually vanished folk community that inspired so many of the early folkies, but grappling instead with the tough, scrawny, red-necked, pig-headed reality of what the modern folk community, for all its faults and failings, really stands for.

Of course, this doesn't sit too well with the instant revolutionaries of the ultra-left, of which Alan Jules Weberman is a devoted member, who find it much simpler and less demanding to people the world with big bad wolves to be offed. So Weberman has formed the Dylan Liberation Front to re-radicalize his hero and get him off his CB (current bag, i.e. heroin). As it becomes clear that Dylan isn't going to be saved from himself that easily, Weberman's invective becomes shriller, more hysterical, more and more turned against Dylan himself.

A recent Weberman article began: 'After studying the life and works of Bob Dylan for five years and after having gained the reputation of the world's leading authority on him, I have come to the conclusion that Dylan has turned into A HYPOCRITE AND A LIAR back in late 1967.'

After listing some of the stocks and real estate upon which he is supposed to have invested his guaranteed earnings from Columbia Records of half a million dollars a year, he exclaims: 'If Dylan thinks he's gonna get away with shit like this that slimey motherfucker is fuckin' crazy.'

Weberman's opinion of Dylan's current writing is scathing: 'Dylan doesn't just "take" money from the hip community by giving his fans groovy records in return for their bread. Instead he rips them off by coming out with shitty music and lyrics, which, on one level, seem to be about true love and how great it is to be straight but which really sing the praises of HEROIN (D's CB) on their metaphorical level ... now I realize that heroin has turned him into a general rip-off artist who uses the reputation of the old groovey right-on Dylan to sell unimaginative, asshole shit to millions of young people. And Zimmerman's scum is paying off – NASHVILLE MAINLINE*, for example, has sold 1,028,770 units, and Bobby gets at least 50 cents a unit.'

So the thing goes on.

It would be laughable were it not for the deadly seriousness of cranks like Weberman, and all the other underprivileged nuts of left and right, the Lee Harvey Oswalds whose names we don't yet know.

The Kennedys weren't killed because of anything they were doing but because, in political terms, they had become superstars. So was Che; the Bolivian SS *had* to murder him, it was their role in the game. So is Mao. Who else? De Gaulle died in his bed – to everyone's surprise. There is some doubt about the nature of Stalin's death. Rudi Dutschke still carries the scars of superstardom on his skull, and he'll never really be well again.

---

*This is a Weberman pun (!). The actual title is 'Nashville Skyline'. Mainlining is injecting a drug direct into a vein, the quickest and toughest way of doing it.

Castro has survived remarkably, for of all the political leaders of today he has accepted the spotlight of his own mass media the most willingly. Mao sends his thoughts out pre-packaged, in little red books; but Fidel goes out on to the streets in person to make speeches lasting for hours of live transmission time on TV, dealing directly, immediately and at length with any questions the people care to raise with him. As a form of direct dialogue this easy access is almost admirable, but as a life insurance policy it is, quite literally, murder.

Or shall we say: suicide?

Jules Siegel wrote of Robert Kennedy in *Rolling Stone:* 'He was a superstar, the heaviest of the superstars, and superstars can't go out in public.

'Never mind the assassins. It was the people he had to fear. They wanted to eat him alive. It was as if the Beatles, at the height of the mania, had walked through the Yankee Stadium shaking hands. It might have been polite and sweet and respectful. Or they might have torn them flesh from bone.

'Anyone who has been in a crowd of people excited by lust should understand the danger. The people are a monster. When they collect in great numbers they become high. They are not used to being high. At the end of a Beach Boys' concert in Indianapolis kids started tearing the seats up and throwing them on stage. For fun. While the Beach Boys were still playing.

'It is possible that the only reason Woodstock was peaceful is that it rained so hard. That was a miracle. There was no miracle at Altamont. There were no surprises.'

McLuhan told Lennon that time in Canada that the reason rock festivals were getting bigger and bigger was because the people were feeling more and more frustrated.

'Frustration creates bigness,' said the sage. 'And when people are frustrated, they feel the need to expand, to get more room and strength ...'

'Frustration releases adrenalin in the system. Adrenalin

creates much bigger muscles and bigger arms and legs and puts tremendous weight on the political body ...

'... The more frustrated people are, the bigger they have to be and the more aggressive they have to be.'

In his chapter on 'Fascist Irrationalism' in 'The Function of the Orgasm', Wilhelm Reich showed how the creation of media superstars like Hitler was the result of individuals' needs to relieve themselves of responsibility for the world around them. 'Passing this responsibility enthusiastically from himself to some Führer or politician has become one of his essential characteristics, since he is no longer able to understand either himself or his institutions, of which he is only afraid. Fundamentally, he is helpless, incapable of freedom, and craving for authority, for he cannot react spontaneously; he is armoured and expects commands, for he is full of contradictions and cannot rely upon himself.'

Out of 31 million voters in March 1933, 17 million voted Hitler into power because, says Reich, they 'felt helpless and incapable of taking the responsibility for the solution of the chaotic social problems within the old political system and frame of thinking.'

Attempts to find the origins of fascism usually rely upon blaming something 'either in the personality of Hitler or in formal political blunders' by his predecessors, thus taking it out of the field of social science and into the realm of individual aberration, but 'In reality, Hitler was only the expression of a tragic conflict in the human masses, the conflict between the longing for freedom and actual fear of freedom'.

This was undoubtedly true, but it is not the whole truth. The violent ends met by both Hitler and Mussolini, as well as Kennedy and the other victims of assassination in the era of the political superstar can be explained only as part of the system of patriarchal, authoritarian government, as a mechanism created by man to help the system function in a way that does not completely destroy subject man's identity. When the priest-king asserted his leadership of the clan collective he was basically a usurper, for the collective had had no need of leaders in the time when every man's hand had to be turned against the common enemies of nature. The concept of leadership was the creation of surplus wealth, for as man began to gain control over his environment, those who controlled this surplus also gained certain rights and privileges. Originally associated with woman, identified with the goodness of nature by virtue of her procreative role, the leadership was first shared with man and then seized by him, resulting in the patriarchal society within which we live today. But the first kings were not merely leaders: originally they had been divine victims, identified with the harvest cut down and buried once a year, only to rise again, and each one must die eventually, that the people might continue to live in plenty.

'The man-god must be killed as soon as he shows symptoms that his powers are going to fail,' wrote Sir James Frazer in 1922, 'and his soul must be transferred to a vigorous successor before it has been seriously impaired by the threatened decay. The advantages of thus putting the man-god to death instead of allowing him to die of old age and disease are, to the savage, obvious enough . . . by slaying him his worshippers could, in the first place, make sure of catching his soul as it escaped and transferring it to a suitable successor; and, in the second place, by putting him to death before his natural force was abated, they would secure that the world should not fall into decay with the decay of the man-god' (The Golden Bough, chapter xxiv).

It may seem strange to describe these children of the electronic age as savages, although it is a charge levelled frequently by their enemies, and the word 'tribes' or 'tribal' is often used when they describe themselves as members of the hip community. But anyway, 'savagery' can be a relative thing, as Le Roi Jones has explained:

L

'So-called nonliterate peoples (called by Western man "primitive") whose languages and therefore whose cultural and traditional histories are not written, are the antithesis of Western man and his highly industrialized civilization. But the idea of "primordial man" or "undeveloped peoples", becomes absurd if we dismiss for a change the assumption that only the ideas and attitudes which the West finds useful or analagous to concepts forwarded within its own system are of any value or profundity. For instance, a highly organized society predicated on the existence of mystical, omniscient superior beings who are in complete control of the lives and fates of all humans might seem a trifle "primitive" if viewed through the eyes of a society whose existence is predicated on exactly opposite hypotheses. . . .

'. . . one of the most persistent traits of the Western white man has always been his fanatical and almost instinctive assumption that his systems and ideas about the world are the most desirable, and further, that people who do not aspire to them, or at least think them admirable, are *savages* or *enemies*. The idea that Western thought might be *exotic* if viewed from another landscape never presents itself to most Westerners' (Blues People).

Not merely is electronic culture creating a new Africa within, it is leading us back to discover the survival of that older Africa, whose rituals continue today, recognizable in many respects as kin to the prehistoric originals. If you doubt that such ceremonies can survive to these enlightened times outside the ranks of cranks and cultists, ask any Englishman why he refuses so definitely to eat horseflesh, a common source of cheap animal protein all over the continent of Europe; then tell him his aversion to horseflesh is because the horse is Britain's totemic beast (as the cow is India's and the pig once was Judaea's), sacred to Epona, the Celtic Demeter. The white horse cut into the chalk hill at Uffington in Berkshire is her symbol. And in the Twelfth Century Giraldus Cambrensis told of the election of a king in Ulster. The ceremony started with the people gathering around a white mare. Then, says Anne Ross in her study, 'Pagan Celtic Britain', the king-elect 'came before the assembled people on his hands and knees, in the manner of an animal, and declares himself to be a beast. The mare is then killed, after his (supposed) sexual union with it, and cooked. The king-elect next sits in the vessel in which the liquid is contained and bathes in the broth and eats the flesh and drinks up the liquid with his mouth.'

Of course, the old rituals do decay as the centuries pass, and if they are revived it is often as ugly caricatures of the old ways. So the growth of literacy and the invention of printing which created the modern state, also inspired a reaction from the peasant survivors of the primitive community, resulting in a revival in the Fourteenth and Fifteenth Centuries and after of the old pre-Christian totemic clans as witchcults, decadent mirror images of the state which was oppressing them. It is no accident that the witch persecutions were intensified after the invention of the printing press and the resulting spread of 'enlightenment', and that the Puritans, theological wing of the industrializing bourgeoisie, were better at witch-finding than the Catholics, for with its survivals of the old matriarchial worship of motherhood, Catholicism left less room for the old religions to manoeuvre. 'This development of an acute witch scare on the basis of the long-standing, chronic system of beliefs was symptomatic of the rapid and fundamental changes the society of Europe was undergoing in its transition from the relatively undifferentiated feudalism of the Middle Ages to the varied, flexible and uncertain social organization that started with the Renaissance and the Reformation,' said Max Marwick in his introduction to 'Witchcraft and Sorcery' in the Penguin series of modern readings of sociology.

We are in a similar transitional society right now, but this time it it away from rather than towards the industrial state which was created by the Renaissance. The sacrificial patriarchs whose deaths marked the growth of man's dictatorship over the earliest class societies are returning as we reverse the process.

These sacrificial victims are the superstars, originally found among political leaders, but as the political system has less and less relevance to our society the victims are sought elsewhere; for instance, in pop music.

In 1965, Phil Ochs expressed doubt of Bob Dylan's ability to survive another year of public performance: 'One year from now I think it will be very dangerous to Dylan's life to get on the stage. In other words, he's gotten inside so many people's heads – Dylan has become part of so many people's psyche, and there're so many screwed-up people in America, and death is such a part of the American scene now. The Kennedy assassination is a part of this story. People are much more conscious of death because when Kennedy was killed, youth was killed, beauty was killed, security was killed . . .

'It's a form of hypnosis. It's not that everybody sits there listening to him with a single-track mind. Dylan has managed to convene a very dangerous neurotic audience together in one place, who are all hipped to him on different levels. They aren't all listening to him in the same way.

'Some of them are there looking for the lost symbol of the message singer. And none of them really understand: none of them have any right to Dylan. Dylan is an individual singing. And these people want to own him. And that's what a lot of Dylan's songs are about: You can't own me – I'm free; you can't own me even though you want to, and you can go to hell – for even trying to own me. And that's absurd – that's a joke – sitting there and saying we want the old Dylan, or we want the new Dylan. That's bullshit, that's nonsense. It's evil. It's a very sick thing going on there. And it's because of this neurotic audience that Dylan has got. And that is why Dylan has got to be careful, and that is why he'll have to quit singing.'

Which is what he did, well within Ochs' deadline,

though it took a motorcycle accident to get him right off the stage. The old Dylan died that day of 'This Wheel's On Fire', and the new one that grew like a phoenix out of the exploding sunburst is cannier than the old, better briefed to survive, though he still uses some of the tricks, like freaking the media to blur the image, making it harder for the marksman to get him in the sights.

His songs wish us all good luck. But for the man exposed, up there on stage, good luck might not possibly be enough.

VIII

The Auto-Destruct Mechanism

"Why don't we do it in the road?"
                    —The Beatles

KNOW WHAT is the greatest single hazard a pop musician has to face? Not drugs, hard or soft. It's travel. A really careful analysis of most pop deaths over the years would show that, in one way or another, modern forms of mechanized transport have killed more pop people than any other single factor.

In one way, this is merely a specific example of the terrible general slaughter that the motor car and the aeroplane have wreaked during the break-up years of our civilization. Any other random sample would probably show the same. When Bessie Smith died in that auto-crash in Mississippi in 1937, one of the best publicized car accidents in the history of pop even before Edward Albee wrote his play about it, there was nothing in particular to distinguish it from any similar black woman's death, including the fact that she died principally because an all-white hospital refused to treat her and they sent her off, bleeding to death to look for one that would. It was something that could have happened to any black woman then or, in a country where the poor have to pay in advance for medical treatment, to any white woman also. The direct correlation that exists between statistics of violent crime and the figures for the ownership of automobiles was working itself out.

But the amount that they have to travel, just to do their work, is incredibly destructive. Straights who think of pop people as long-haired layabouts should try it out for size some time. The sheer physical labour of it would cripple them.

Touring! The Grand Tour used to be the elegant way of seeing the world but today it means a long hard grind of motorway or freeway or autobahn travel in a Ford Transit truck, greasy meals snatched in transport cafes, endless hassles getting the equipment set up, from changing power plugs and even transformers to fit in with the local supply to wrestling ten feet high column speakers on to the corners of the stage, balancing the sound . . . all that before the band starts playing.

After this gruelling toil, they are expected to create, to put on a show, to *swing* so the kids, who may be students or just locals for whom this hop is the only bright spot in their week of evenings, can groove and leap about. And if they play as tired as they feel, the cognoscenti label them another record company hype and the word gets round. They stay away next time.

The crowd goes home at midnight or thereabouts, possibly later, but whenever it is, for the band the night is only just begun, for they have to load the gear back into the van and drive it somewhere – perhaps a few miles to the nearest hotel, or all the way home. In America it's worse, except that they use planes instead of Transits. Joe Cocker's film of 'Mad Dogs and Englishmen' gives some idea of what it's like.

True, a lot of the physical work is properly the task of the roadie, the grandly-titled road manager who for only

£15 to £20 a week (even with a big name group) has to do most of the lifting and shifting as well as the driving. During the show, too, he may double as sound balancer, in which case he is still working almost as hard as they, keeping an eye on the output meters to see they don't peak too often and distort, sipping the single pint he knows must last the night out or he'll be over the central reservation of the M1 before he can say 'multiple pile-up', and another band's obituary is a paragraph in black type on page 4 of the *Melody Maker*.

Even so, while the band is flopped out in the back of the truck, rarely but occasionally making it with one or two of those groupies we've heard so much about, the roadie's still working, and even without the beer he may find it hard to stay awake.

The musicians struggle against the grind of touring, the one-night stands that have them darting back and forth across the map like maddened mosquitoes, but as the business is at present constituted, it's hard to avoid it. I've heard it from so many of them, how they're only going to do concerts now, and I know it isn't merely because a decent hall can hold well over a thousand compared with a few hundred in a club (in America the difference is much greater, proportionately) and all of them are listening much more intently than you can in a ballroom. It isn't even because of the acoustics (many concert halls are as unsuitable for rock as ballrooms would be for symphony concerts). What is attractive about the concert halls is that there just aren't that many of them, and the money is much better, so that in Britain a band will do a tour which consists of a series of concert dates, then lay off and lie around for a while, recuperating.

It doesn't work, though, because the type of contact you can get with a concert hall audience is so out of context with pop media. This sitting around on plush seats listening so carefully to the music, listening to every nuance like it was Mozart, then doling out the appropriate ration of applause, creates the sort of search for 'excellence' that Lennon complains about in so much modern rock, the illusion that they are artists, creating for posterity, not hired hands playing for that instant alone. The sort of rock which will create a good response in a concert situation is probably not very good rock, though it may please the critics on the posh Sunday newspapers.

As Pete Townshend of the Who has said so many times, touring is essential for a rock band – if it is to continue to be a rock band.

The audience response you can get in a club is something else, even though nobody outside a lunatic fringe (a spastic crowd who have been dubbed idiot dancers by the cooler fraternity) dances any more, at least not at the time of writing. The sound is rarely as good as the cheapest stereo systems the kids have at home, producing an all-over blur which is much closer to the woodshed sound those 1950s recordings used to have, forcing a form of musical communication which will cut through it, incisively. But the communication from audience to band is better, too, at a physical level, where body signals take over from clever verbalizing and the band can tell how well they are playing by watching the way the punters move their bodies.

To get this, you can't get away from travelling, physically. The distribution network for records is much more efficient than it used to be, and you don't have to be on a 'major' label to have your product sold in Wigan or Dubuque, but the system lacks feedback, that report back from the periphery to the control centre which is essential to all cybernetic systems, according to Norbert Wiener. The closest thing to feedback the industry has are the charts, telling how the various singles or albums are selling, and it is this need for feedback which keeps the charts going, even though everyone in the industry laughs at them, knows they are unreliable and easily influenced by promoters willing to invest a hundred quid on buying discs from the right shops on the panel. But the charts don't tell which cuts on an album get played the most, or why a listener likes that solo and not the ensemble that follows immediately after, or even if the customer bought the record unheard because of its reputation (ie its chart position) and hated it from the first time he played it.

Only on the road can the musicians get this sort of positive and negative response, which is why when they become big enough to stay home and concentrate upon recordings something goes out of their music. It happened to the Beatles. It's why their white album and 'Abbey Road' and 'Get Back' are so soulless, and why until the actual break-up became inevitable they kept talking about making at least one more live appearance, just to show they could do it. It's why Dylan came out of retirement, why the Stones went on the road again before splitting for the south of France. And it's why there are still rumours that the Beatles will re-form, with Klaus Voorman who did the sleeve of 'Revolver' on bass instead of Paul, though we all really know, don't we, that it'll never happen, ever.

The electronic media's creation of the global village, McLuhan's utopian vision of the collective founded upon instant communication, has taken us just so far. Then it stopped. We can communicate with each other on a one-to-one basis by telephone or on a one-to-many basis by TV, radio or gramophone records. But we cannot communicate many-to-one except by the ballot box and the similarly obsolete mechanics of the marketplace, still less can we communicate many-to-many, unless we are actually in physical contact with each other.

Hence the big rock festivals, which if they are exercises in frustration, as McLuhan says, that must be because we know there's a hell of a lot of us but we just can't believe it unless we see ourselves all in one spot. I mean, if we can push a Frank Zappa record or a Fairport Convention record or an Elton John record or a James Taylor record into the charts without hardly ever hearing it on the radio (especially in Britain), paranoia can begin to set in fairly soon. You begin to wonder if the whole thing isn't a figment of the imagination after all, and you are the only freak in creation who digs the sound coming out of the speakers.

Even a jam-packed Albert Hall concert with all 5,000 seats full (which is virtually impossible, thanks to the feudal system of seat ownership instituted in Queen Victoria's day, thus ensuring that there are always some seats empty at even the most popular event) doesn't give you the same buzz as being one of 50,000, or one of 100,000, hey what about being one of a quarter of a million people sitting out there cool in the sunny grass and living the way you want to live unmindful of fuzz or straight neighbours telling you turn it down or uptight bosses and schoolteachers. The nicest thing about those crowd scenes in 'Woodstock', when the camera pulls back and that grainy 16mm-blown-up-to-70mm film image fills the whole screen, is the incredible variety of activity. These quarter of a million people are no Nuremberg rally. Each one is doing something different.

The hope that such a scene engenders is dangerous, however, which is what happened at Altamont, the stock-car racing track where the Rolling Stones gave their disastrous free concert at the end of 1969. It is at such times that the hip media reveal themselves as the true heirs of the transitional technology that spawned the yellow press; the same combination of print logic, with a university accent, plus telegraphic immediacy produces similar faults and strengths.

Like the best of the straight press, they can rise to an emergency with the sort of in-depth coverage that wins Pulitzer Prizes. But they also tend to reduce all events into simple one plus two equals three linear equations, so that when they go seeking basic causes and people to blame (that there is always someone individually or collectively to blame for everything is a basic principle of yellow journalism) their conclusions are not merely invalid, but because they are chasing after phantoms they leave the reader worse advised than before. If anything bad happens, they argue, there's got to be someone wicked behind it, whether it be trigger-happy pig cops or superstar rock musicians, and any suggestion that the bad things arose out of something basically groovy, that the one cannot be had without the other, a total deal, is treated as a sophistic cop-out.

The hip media really went to town at Altamont. They were already sore about the high prices the Stones had been charging for their regular concerts across America, so that the idea of a free concert (just one free concert, tucked away on the West Coast, for the whole of the great big US of A) sounded a lot like window dressing to them. They didn't say as many cruel things about Woodstock though people died there too, although you couldn't exactly call it murder.

But wait a minute, didn't the Oakland jury find Alan Passaro not guilty of stabbing Meredith Hunter to death at Altamont? Well, yes, that's another good old American newspaper tradition that the hip media have inherited, that a man is guilty, so far as the press is concerned, as soon as he is charged, added to which the hip media reserve the right to continue to write about him as if he's guilty long after he's been acquitted.

And not only him, but also people who weren't even on trial. Sam Cutler, who hired the 300 Hells Angels to police the Altamont crowd and paid them with five hundred dollars' worth of booze, Jagger for the manner of his performance, and even the local police department for not rushing into the fray at Altamont, clubs swinging, to sort it all out.

How's that again? Here's all this talk of an alternative community, of the systems we are setting up, of how, basically, we could manage our affairs without any interference from the straight state, and that interference is the only thing that's hanging us up, and then they want to pillory Sheriff Frank Madigan and his eight deputies because they didn't interfere, because when they got to the scene of the crime they took one look at the 300,000 kids milling about and split, but fast.

The underground's very own super-capitalist, Bill Graham, went further. He said not merely that the law should have stepped right in and caught the murderer then and there, but that they should have banned the concert before it happened. 'Sometimes force is valid,' he said. 'They should have taken Mr Jagger, twisted his fucking arms behind his back, put him in front of a radio, and said, "Mr Jagger, if we have to break your arm, call it off".'

Truly has it been said that inside many long-haired freaks are short-haired straights screaming to get out and stomp on someone.

Through all the charges and counter-charges some truth emerges, but it has been largely ignored because it doesn't help to deliver a neatly parcelled villain up to the media chopping block for sentence and execution. We can accept that Altamont was organized at too short a notice, and that the Stones management were incredibly naïf in thinking they could hire Hells Angels to police the event for them. They had used the British Angels in Hyde Park with very little bother, but then the British Angels . . . it isn't the same thing.

In neutral, socio-anthropological terms, the Angels make a fascinating study, with their remarkable clan loyalty, the almost medieval rigidity of their code of knightly conduct, the anti-morality of their obsessive dirtiness and general nastiness, like a chapter from 'Story of O' re-written for 'Classics Illustrated'. And they are truly tribal, which few of the rest of us can claim in this age of supposedly reviving tribalism.

The fact remains, however, that very few of us would be wise to try to number a genuine Angel as a friend, if only because their rigid code makes it impossible to function at all except on their own terms – which is difficult unless you happen to know all their rules. Just not knowing one rule can be, literally, fatal. Ignorance of the law is no excuse.

And apart from all this, the fact remains that if you give *anyone* a cop's job, he's going to act like a cop, whether he wears a uniform or not. Asking anyone to police your event, whether it is Ron Foulkes hiring Securicor for Isle of Wight or Sam Cutler inviting the Angels to become dictators of Altamont, is just the same as handing yourself over to the law. Don't go all utopian on us and say you're so self-disciplined you don't need the official law, when you're just using different people and calling them something else, because they're still law.

It is so generally accepted that you have to have someone, for God's sake, to keep people off stage and stop them scragging the talent, that the thing becomes an end in itself. At cash events, of course, there's a reason: to stop people getting in for free, or into a more privileged position than they have paid for. At Isle of Wight there was this beautiful chick who took off her clothes and ran on to the no-mans-land in front of the stage and danced there, naked, to the music of Edgar Broughton. Beautiful. But, they say, what would happen if everyone did it? (which is what they have been saying to me all my life, ever since I first asked for special permission to do something just a little bit unorthdox at school, now I can't remember exactly what, but it surely was something no one else would want to do, like doing 'Ulysses' as my set book instead of John Galsworthy, so they said No. Ever since, I don't bother to ask, so they can't refuse). So the last scene in that particular movie is the guy picking her up and carrying her nakedness off, all kicking arms and legs. It wasn't so much her nudity they objected to, I understand, as her cheek in violating the sacred area in front of stage reserved for VIPs and photographers. That was that same festival when Al Grossman kept 40 vacant seats in the VIP enclosure marked 'Mr Bob Dylan's party' – and didn't use half of them.

What made the Isle of Wight incident all the more ludicrous was the fact that Broughton makes a practice of inviting people up on to the stage to groove with him, and he gets some aggro from commissionaires and similar flunkies for this. He has been banned by some universities for the habit, especially the one where the stage collapsed.

The people whose life's work it is to prevent such untoward goings on are known in the music business as 'jobsworths' because of their tendency, when faced with the unusual or anything else demanding individual judgement or initiative, to say: 'Sorry, guv, but it's more than me job's worth.'

In even the most benevolent situation, the guy who agrees to police the actions of his fellow men, or worse still he who volunteers, has got to have some kink of megalomania in there somewhere. It's a humane variant of Catch 22: Anyone who is willing to do the job is automatically disqualified. The only person fit to do the job is the one who refuses to.

The idea of using the Angels, of all people, as cops is really ludicrous, for though the Angels may be many things, and they are a far from simple phenomenon, guardians of the hip community they're certainly not. The fact that, as fellow freaks, they are equally persecuted by the state doesn't necessarily make them allies. There is no such thing as association by guilt.

Ask the peace marchers of the Vietnam Day Committee in Berkeley, California, who were attacked by the Oakland chapter of Hells Angels in 1965 – some said with the connivance of the Oakland law. Altamont is in Oakland. The Angels were led on that occasion by Sonny Barger. He led them at Altamont, too.

Young Republican Clubs passed resolutions praising them for their patriotism back then and a Mr Fred Ullner, director of Republicans for Conservative Action, formed an organization called Friends of Hells Angels to raise bail for any who were arrested while out stomping Commies. One of the first recipients of this bounty: Sonny Barger.

It's not so much that the Angels are really Nazis, despite their love of Nazi symbols, which are worn chiefly to get people uptight. When they helped Hitler's American Sons break the strike at the Colony Furniture Co. of Richmond, Calif., after they had finished stomping strikers, the Angels turned round and stomped the fascists too, for good measure.

The Angels are just mean.

Not in Mick Jagger's son-of-Satan let's pretend way, ogle ogle kiss kiss slap slap. *Really* mean. So when they were brought in to guard the stage, that meant it was their stage, right? Not the Stones' stage; certainly not the Jefferson Airplane's. They're a *true* tribe, man, not taken in by any of this superstar shit. Airplane member Marty Balin got stomped on when he tried to curb them and he lay bleeding at stage front, unconscious, while the band played on. The song Grace Slick was singing at the time was 'That's the Other Side of This Life'.

But it wasn't merely Angel meanness. That was a nasty crowd they had to deal with, bum trips and screaming freaks, surging and waiting to explode. The atmosphere was very strange, supercharged with electric evil. All the bad vibes that had emanated from Jagger since 'Their Satanic Majesties' seemed to have gathered over the Altamont Speedway. Astrology freaks pointed with trembling fingers at the moon in Scorpio, closed their eyes, and feared the worst.

The trouble really happened when the Stones got into 'Sympathy for the Devil'. 'We always have something very funny happen when we start that number,' said Jagger as the band stopped. The loaded billiard cues the Angels were using for riot control clubs rose and fell. There were calls from the stage for doctors, though earlier Cutler had

M

refused to broadcast appeals for help for people on bum acid trips. Jagger staggered about, visibly bewildered, alternating between appeals to reason and threats to split if the people didn't cool it out, both equally vain.

But the alchemy was working. The witch bottle finally exploded during 'Under My Thumb', whose evil chord sequence seemed, in that context, to epitomize sado-sexual horrors. The band stopped again. Jagger had seen this black dude in the pale green suit jump up, seen him pull a gun, seen the Angels pounce, saw the black man turn and flee, the Angel's knife hand rising and falling upon his back. Then the crowd surged back, like sea smoothing disturbed sand on a beach.

Meredith Hunter, an 18-years-old paranoid black speed freak who carried a gun for self-defence whenever he was in big crowds, fell, stomped and stabbed to death. Later the Coroner pronounced that he died of shock and haemorrhage due to multiple wounds in the back, a wound on the left side of his forehead and another on the right side of his neck.

His white girlfriend, Patty, said the Angels took Hunter's gun away. There is some doubt that the weapon produced at Alan Passaro's trial was actually the same gun, though it was the same type, a .22 Smith and Wesson, and it came, presumably, from the Angels. They told the law they would leave it on a porch to be found, and there it was one morning, the right kind at least. No prints, of course.

But the Angels said that Hunter actually fired the gun at Jagger and though no slug was found, there is a flash that could be a gunshot in the film record that exists of the killing. All you can hear is the band playing. However, the law testified that the gun they produced in evidence hadn't been fired for years.

Mysteries.

The whole thing begins to have as many intricate implications within complications as the JFK assassination.

Who, for instance, was the young guy who ran up to Mick Jagger as he got out of the KFRC radio station's helicopter, shouting words of hatred, and punched Jagger in the face? Was he just a 'crazed freak' as *Rolling Stone* called him? Well, was he? We don't even know his name.

Between then – it was mid-afternoon – and the Stones' appearance on stage at dusk, Jagger had been the victim of five more attempts at violence. The Meredith Hunter incident made it a grand total of seven attacks.

And the superstar mystique had been building up as the minutes clocked by. For one thing the stage was kept empty for 75 minutes, as the evening fell, while the Stones waited for the magic to get stronger. Medical teams appealed for the lights to be turned up but someone said no. They worked on in the gathering dark. The crowd shifted, uneasily.

And then the Stones were on. 'Jumping Jack Flash.' 'Carol.' 'Sympathy for the Devil.' 'Under My Thumb.' And Hunter goes down. By the time the medics got to him, it was probably already too late. In Vietnam, with immediate intravenous transfusions, he might have survived. Altamont didn't have those sort of facilities. Altamont had hardly any facilities.

It's all there on film, the Rolling Stones' 'Gimme Shelter' the savage testament to another 'free' show. Free? As in Hyde Park, the free show was really just a monstrous film set for a movie about the Stones and the groovy vibrations that day in early December 1969. They had plans for a rush release by March of the following year though Altamont was actually a year old before it got out.

What would the Stones do? They'd lost the 'good vibrations' script somewhere down there in the blood and the shit. Everyone knew the killing had been filmed. Would it be in the movie? It was; first run at normal speed, then freeze-frame by freeze-frame like any other assassination. Which is what it seems to be, in the movie: an assassination attempt that didn't come off, thanks to an out-of-work barber in Angel colours who pounced with a knife and killed the man with the gun before he had time to fire.

Whether that is what it actually was is less important than the fact that it is so easy to believe that Jagger had to die, had been due for it for a long time, had been grooming himself for the role of primal man ever since he wrested leadership of the band from sweet little Brian Jones, the randy little fucker who spent so much time coping with paternity suits, Brian who was already dead before Altamont, who died just before Hyde Park when Mick read us Shelley, shushing the noisy crowd, and then they released thousands of butterflies into the sky above us and it was beautiful. But Mick had edged Brian out, long before all the pills and stuff had bombed him as a performer, that time they recorded in America without him. Though he didn't seem so important to the band by then, and some of their finest music was made just before and just after he left, the Stones' days were numbered. They became Mick's band, and the South of France started beckoning. Only a matter of time.

The Jagger legend, which had started as a press agent's hype, had grown and grown. The devil incarnate. Please allow me to introduce myself. 'We always have something very funny happen when we start that number.' Hope you guess my name. Lucifer, I'm in need of some restraint. Jagger really believes it. He is the devil. Or really, he's the only one around who realizes we are all devils, especially the saints. It's the story of 'Performance', the terrifyingly autobiographical movie the distributors were scared to release, with Turner the fading rock star and Chas the vicious Soho tearaway changing places and roles. '*As heads is tails*' and yin is yang, the Manicheist heresy from the Third Century, suppressed so bloodily three centuries later but rooted still in the dualism of the great mystic philosophers, from Plato to Rimbaud.

The mixture of good and evil runs right through the whole song. Lucifer is there when Jesus '*had his moment of doubt and faith'* and makes sure that Pilate plays his appointed role. To Bob Dylan's question, was it Jesus or Judas had God on his side, Jagger answers: Both.

He was there in the fighting of World War II, when the bodies stank – the liberation of the camps? For if war is evil, what does that make the liberation?

The Russian Revolution is treated in the same equivocal fashion. Lucifer turns up in St Petersburg because it's time for a change (presumably 'good'). And the architect of change murders the Tsars family horribly. 'Good?'

Ewan MacColl told me he once asked Jagger if he was saying the murder of the Tsar was a bad thing, betraying such a failure to appreciate the basic nature of the song that I'm surprised Jagger bothered to answer him at all, it's such a dumb question, for that's what the song's saying: what is 'good'? What is 'bad'? Can good ends come from bad means? Or are the terms meaningless?

Jagger said he thought the murder was 'bad', no doubt confirming MacColl in his prejudgement that, for all of his 'Street Fighting Man' talk, Jagger was basically a counter-revolutionary.

So he is, for without counter-revolution, argues Lucifer, how can there be a revolution?

This ambiguity extends to Jagger's physical presence, the pouting, girl-like gestures, the fag waving, the sexuality which is so explicit, no more subtle than a stripper's bump and grind, and yet still leaves a nagging doubt.

A critic reviewing 'Gimme Shelter' caught this exactly in his description: 'He hits the crowd with his pelvis, flings his scarf around his shoulders, jabs nervously at his flowing hair, mouths like a woman in heat, jerks with an aggressive, staccato beat that is as explicit as an anatomy chart. The ambiguity of his sex, the spectacle of raper and victim in one body, threw the witnesses into convulsions of excitement.'

Back in the days of his promo films for 'I Can't Get No

Satisfaction' he used to do the face-slapping mime, his hand going back and forth in front of him the way he always does, in time with Charlie Watts' drums, crash crash, crash-crash-crash. Marat and de Sade in one.

Long-stem roses hit the stage. You'd think he was Judy Garland singing 'Over the Rainbow'.

But the roses and the bullet from Meredith Hunter's gun are, basically, moved by the same impulse: they are the tribute due to a superstar. *'I shouted out "Who killed the Kennedys" when after all it was you and me.'* The rose becomes a bullet, or the bullet is a rose, the ultimate dualism. Jagger's destiny had become the intersection of two vectors. Inevitably, when the two lines met, would come the exploding rose of blood from the temples, the end (or a beginning?).

On stage, Jagger is big enough for this myth, but off-stage it becomes too heavy. He is a little too small, a little too human. So he chickened off to the Riviera, a Hollywood wedding to a recording industry tycoon's girlfriend, with the French rights to Rolling Stones records as part of the settlement, before it was too late, before the myth completely dominated his private life as well and set the auto-destruct mechanism working.

I believe this is what happened to Jimi Hendrix and Janis Joplin, whose deaths, separated by less than a month in time, shook the whole of rock and showed us that we had really come to the end of the superstar era. They both came on as powerful stage presences, both aggressively sexual, but off-stage they were both gentle, vulnerable people who were oppressed by the monster that inhabited them on stage. Of course, the stage presence was based on something they dredged out of themselves, the clothes were already in their wardrobes, for both were incredible studs (the only word for Janis, whose attitude to sex was very male) and it was this that was the foundation for much of what they did.

From here on, however, they differed, for while Janis

was virtually one-dimensional professionally, there was a contradiction within the Hendrix stage presence, between the rhapsodic melodies he would play, even picking them out with his teeth, even when they were runs at breakneck speed, and the aggressive black superstud he created to people the fantasies of the white audience. Occasionally the two would unite, as his pink tongue flickered in and out, lizardlike, between the black lips in time to a hammered-on B. B. King-style tremolo with the right hand (he played guitar left-handed), the tongue giving even such a simple musical trick a sexual connotation, the left hand held free to show the guitar was working on its own, the neck surging and throbbing captive in his right hand like a massive member (and Jimi was reputed to be extremely well-hung). Was it accident that if you play a Fender Stratocaster upside down, as Jimi did, the strange convolutions of the head, with the machine heads hidden down what has become the straight lower side, look remarkably like a cock with the foreskin pulled back?

The lyrics of his songs were full of desperate longing, a yearning for something better that he summed up, at almost the end of his life, by the anguished rendering of 'The Star-Spangled Banner' which he played at Woodstock. As a political statement of the American dream viewed by the man part black part red, it had such incredible power that his murmured comment, 'Well, we're all Americans, aren't we? I'm just playing it the way music is in the air these days, and there's lots of static, or hadn't you noticed?' was almost superfluous. Except that in America, of all countries outside Nazi Germany, the flag and other national symbols are treated with such exaggerated respect, they are so sacred, that a mod who makes himself a Stars and Stripes jacket, as Pete Townshend did with the Union Jack, is asking for trouble. A girl who used to walk around with an unviolated star-spangled banner round her shoulders got stomped by the local law and although everyone agreed it was a bit strong, beating up a chick like that, on the other hand, after all it was, you know, the flag?

When I first saw 'Hair', in New York, the 99 per cent straight audience (Madison Avenue hip in their Cardin double-breasted suits and long sideburns, but basically straight for all that) took all the talk of dope and homosexuality and masturbation with amused toleration. But the section, 'Folding the Flag', which pokes very gentle fun at flag worship, had them all sitting bolt upright in their seats. These hippies better know that there are still limits beyond which it's safer not to step, sonofabitch. And they didn't. The sigh of relief, the relaxation in the theatre, was almost audible.

There is all of that in Hendrix's 'Star Spangled Banner'. But if you see this incredible performance in its context something else emerges which doesn't nullify the political statement, not at all, but adds a very personal commentary.

At the time of Woodstock, Hendrix was very much the passenger of his own legend. Having created incredible tone-colours and unbelievable sounds with just guitar, bass and drums, often recording with virtually no overdubs, he had split from the two English boys who had such a rapport with him, and formed a new band of superstars, the Buddha of percussion, Buddy Miles, on drums. To be frank, it wasn't working out.

Out of the money he was making, he tried to realize this dream that others before him had had, of a studio in Greenwich Village where everything was cool, dedicated to the creative abilities of the musicians, where that was all that would count. It was the dream of Apple, which failed. And of Dylan's basement, which worked, because it was so simple, and just a few guys were involved.

Setting up Electric Ladyland really screwed Hendrix up, for here you have this gentle, unworldly cat, so vulnerable, trying to buck the whole East Coast establishment on his ownsome, and succeeding to a certain extent. But it really wasn't his trip, any more than being a paratrooper had been his trip. He had made it for 25 drops out of 26. Could he make it this time?

He echoed the sentiments of so many other more moderately endowed performers when he told film-maker Austin John Marshall right back in the early days of 'Are You Experienced?': 'I just wish we could make records regardless of length or what we say in them. I just wish we could just make them without worrying about censorship or worrying about this or worrying about that. From now on I just think we're going to be making exactly what we're trying to say and if it gets censored, well it's just too bad.'

The impossible dream of the pop musician, who is rooted right into the heart of the money system, who depends upon it for things like amplification equipment, for transportation, for studio facilities, for record marketing organization, hoping that one day he'll be able to create another structure that's independent of the money men. And when he does it, he has to hire a money man to run it. And the more successful he is, the more the original concept is destroyed.

Jimi told Marshall a science fiction fable about the origin of the rings of Saturn which turns the process into myth: 'Saturn was like earth was today, you know, with people and stuff, you know, scenes. And there's one type of person that really don't dig these other type of people, something like human beings are now, you know, how they might move up to the suburbs or something like that, or if one of them moves next door to them they might leave altogether, for instance.

'But this is in a nice way because these smart people here, they could paint really nice and they're artists and craftsmen and they can do all sorts of things. The other people just laid about.

'So they finally got their own planet together, their own scene together on one of the largest moons that circles round Saturn. They got about two or three hundred years pass and they really have a nice civilization. They don't have no tall buildings. Everything is ... they got everything together that they need there. I can't explain it now because I get too worked up.

'Anyway, all these other people, those really rough people down there on Saturn, say: "I don't know about those people. They must really think they're smart" or something like that, you know.

'So they started little cold wars and all this is going on within three or four or five hundred years in time, and finally the people down there, they shot a rocket up and blew up the planet.

'The idea of these people trying to do good because they was trying to make it nice for the people on the planet, you know, on Saturn. But then the people on the planet got very jealous after a few years and blew this place up. There was a big war went on. Then finally at the end they blew it up completely and it's circling round and round by the gravitational pull.

'Yeah, but each of the fragments represents a halo for those people trying to do good for the people on Saturn.'

To people who saw Jimi only as the big bad nigger hiding in imagination under the white girls' beds, going to jump out and *git* them and fuck them rotten, this gentle story should be a revelation. Or would it be? Would they, like the Yorkshire businessman who saw Jagger in the restaurant, reject the evidence in favour of the myth they were familiar with? After all, Jimi's sexy come-on on stage was so obviously just an act, so patently absurd most of the time, that if you could really take it seriously, if you could believe it was really him, you'd believe anything.

It is significant, though, that in Jimi's story the 'rough people' who lay around doing nothing creative are the *others*. Being a pop musician is not merely very taxing psychologically, it is also bloody hard work, physically.

Also, Jimi's complicated racial background, the largely

white education that made it so easy for him to parody white fantasies of black sexual potency, made him an outsider among his own kind. At the end of 'I Don't Live Today' the song collapses into science fiction chaos, and Jimi's voice comes howling across the stereo like a disembodied spirit: 'Ohh-h, there ain't no life nowhere.'

The white scene loved Hendrix as a visual experience because he took all *their* things and made them somehow foreign. Lillian Roth, of the *Sidney Morning Herald*, wrote: 'That was a big summer for Carnaby Street and he was wearing and buying what were then new and very English clothes – velvet jackets, floral frilled shirts, tight, tight pants with belled cuffs. He was the first *black* man to dress like an English fop and an Eighteenth Century dandy. Too much.

'The English, to whom black men were still a novelty and wildly erotic and somehow tied up with the whole rock explosion, went quietly berserk. The Americans, for whom black faces were commonplace, thought it was the gear, tied as it was to the Beatles and English groups, that was the novelty and erotic . . .

'. . . A huge abyss had sprung up between whites and blacks (even young whites and young blacks) in the few years before he came along. When rock happened, even though it came straight out of black music, it and the Beatles and Carnaby Street and swinging London were still basically a white experience. Jimi walked into that phenomenon wearing the white man's clothes as a kind of peace offering and gesture of friendship. His Carnaby Street shirts were like an extended hand. Then he promptly made the clothes his so that after that, all the extravagance on whites began to look like just another black imitation. Today young black men have almost completely taken over the look and I'm not even talking about the hair and how Jimi made it possible for black men to have, symbolically anyway, long hair; and not only black men but all the white men whose hair was too curly to grow suddenly took courage from him and grew dandelion heads of their own . . .'

Sounds nice and easy, but Jimi got a lot of static from his own people: 'I feel almost completely lost now, sometimes, you know from almost anything because when I was staying in Harlem, you know, I used to go in the clubs and my hair was very long. Sometimes I might tie it up or do something with it. Cats say: "Look at that black Jesus" or "What's this supposed to be?" God, even in your own section. I mean, I had friends with me in Harlem, 125th Street, when we're walking down the street cats, girls, old girls saying "Oo-ooh, what's this, a circus or something?" '

All this was there in 'Star-Spangled Banner'. The movie doesn't show it but actually Jimi just had not been able to get it on at that point. On the sound track album it's closer to the reality of what happened: a messy jam at first, leading nowhere. Hendrix says, interrupting the music as if some sort of apology were called for: 'You can leave it you want to. We're just jamming, that's all.' The music doodles on, including some nice things such as Jimi could always produce even in the middle of the worst bummers, and then, suddenly . . . an act of desperation!

'Star-Spangled Banner.' A tour de force that electrifies the whole thing, turning it on to a new artistic dimension. Here the movie tells what the record can't, the physical contortions necessary to produce those contorted sounds, the painful grimaces of a man tearing something out of his soul, a man tortured by dying – or by the equally traumatic experience of birth.

Then, the thing out of his system, he relaxes into 'Purple Haze'. He has paid his artistic dues.

The only time I ever met Janis Joplin was at the Newport Folk Festival in 1968. She was undoubted queen of the show. And she spent so much time balling with the young man from the Elektra publicity department, back in his room at the Viking Hotel, that she was really hard to locate. I had to have an interview, so I finally cornered her at one of the parties George Wein used to throw after the Festival closed each night, finding her sitting in the corner of the room among her cronies, looking lost, drinking Jack Daniels.

We went outside on to the steps of the wooden frame house to talk, in the soft Rhode Island night, of her childhood, dealing dope in college, the influence of Leadbelly (a part of the story that somehow didn't have the ring of truth about it, sounding like something Grossman told her to say), how her family didn't care what she was doing so long as she was a success at it, the sort of irrelevant relevancies of public and private information out of which modern pop journalism is constructed.

Peter Seeger's wife Toshi came up to talk about a radio programme I was helping to put together as a memorial to Woody Guthrie. I wanted Pete's reminiscences of Woody on tape but he was just as hard to get into a quiet place as Janis, though for different reasons.

Now Toshi is a beautiful Japanese-American woman, a tower of strength and God's right arm to Peter, but she surely isn't someone you can dismiss or get away from after a sentence or two. What she had to say was going to be said and there was no stopping her. She went on to talk about her daughter, just arrested in Mexico, and she was flying down next day to try and get her out of jail. After a minute Janis said, rather choked, 'You don't seem very interested in what I've got to say' and she split back into the house to the booze and the music and her friends.

It wasn't haughty, you know, the superstar saying who is this Oriental gook interrupting my interview with the Melody Maker of London, England? She was really hurt. And as soon as I finished with Toshi I tracked Janis down and apologized, eating crow perhaps excessively to salve that bruised self-confidence.

A week later I saw the band, Big Brother and the Holding Company, unloading the gear outside a TV studio in New York. I enquired of Sam, the guitarist, after Janis (I never heard anyone ever call her Pearl, which they say is her nickname). She was coming on later so I asked the band to say hello to her for me.

I hope they passed on the message, because I never saw her again.

EPILOGUE

The Last Sacrament
(from a longer sequence)

When we forgot the way to be a god
we made us kings
and searched their entrails for the truth
somehow we mislaid
when priests stood separate from the lonely crowd.

That was when
you could still hear the old tongue
from Connemara east to Asia Minor
singing the same we sang
across the plains from India,
shattered, fragmented by catastrophe,
the blood we drank dying on our tongues
after the last savage verse died
in the god's torn throat.

It is so long
and I have so many dreams.
Sometimes I imagine
Prometheus never gave us fire.

We were no more humble then than now
for we were sons of kings,
proud to rule the seasoned earth
with our love and death,
quick to joy and anger both,
large-eyed, red-haired, long-moustached,
turning the sky into an hour-glass
whose sands slipped through a crab-shaped hole in space
they saw from China
before the Norman bastard came to rape my goddess wives.

We planted calculating stones like trees on hills
and on Salisbury plain I tended sacred flocks
until a holy lamb should bleed for us again,
and every winter plucked the flowering thorn
grown from his promised corpse
beside the wattle church he planted when a child.

Like Blake, I knew the lamb was dead.
An eagle flew skew-wise across my heaven,
shitting roads along my lines of power the swallows know,
damming our streams with cities,
poisoning them at source,
running chemicals into our wells
where slaughtered horses turned red eyes
up to the jews-harp clouds of flies

The sulphur filled my bardic throat with smoke
and all I croaked
were memories of Adam's fall.

Their legions marched us into mists of cyanide
and piled our garbage bones up
for the liberating bulldozers.
They squirted DDT into our sleeves
and pulled our pants down
to squeeze the pus out of our cocks.
Parted our women's lips,
seeking for coins, or crabs.

The noonday dark enfolded us in smog
at dead of day,
so black our clawing hands before our faces
could only sense the grey unhappiness we touched.

I learnt to hate those squawking eagles with their bundled
     canes
whose suns dance widdershins across the scarlet earth.
I spit in the eye of their hurricane
and wipe the returned phlegm away
upon my ragged harpist's sleeve
and spit again
finding more gob
even from the fist that unroots my teeth.

With Ned Ludd we hammered down
the frames they put around my working day.
The shuttles chattered all our names
in numbered ledger talk
until we broke their tongues out,
winding their yarns about us like Maypole strands.

I scraped Mons mud from the boots I wore all winter
and hung my helmet on a dead man's foot.
We cursed both generals
and climbed one sandbagged Christmas from our graves
to sport with sun in the village we created
between the scribbled wires.
Next year we choked upon each other's gas
and a skull rolled between our crater goalposts.

How many of us died those four French years
and how many of our songs froze on our grinning lips!
In taverns whores administered our last communions:
each May was bitter like a hawthorn frost beside the hearth.

October blossomed poppies on their squares of cities
and in the snow once more we murdered kings.
The harvest failed

N

and the factory masters promised help
to screw the steppes with motor tractor stations.
They gave us deeds of ownership
to gearwheels.
We kept them turning through the hardest winters
burning up our blood so fast for future promise
today's deceit went undiscovered.

We thought we were different from other factory folk
but the same oilsmoke clogged our songs,
the same cogs intermeshed and mashed our minds,
the same coins leaded down our legs
though prices rose like factory chimneytops.

When they charged us with betrayal
it was easy to admit
that indeed each one of us had comrades who had died
to build more slaughterhouse Chicagos
under the red flags upon their graves.

The queues to see the wax men lengthened,
seeking a god who'd rise, like corn again,
to bring the autumn spring of revolution back.
They took the hard man out and hid his bones
to quiet rumours of the things they'd done that bore his
      name.
In London, the reading room in Bloomsbury gathered dust:
new rebels studied change
with gramophones.

And so we have survived
perhaps to start the sequence up again
preserving our human kind against the steel of thieves.

. . . now I stand,
a penman when the ink runs dry,
carving instead into our lives
the hieroglyphic truth I seek
as history unwinds itself

to bring again the time of gods.

. . .

We are unlearning
what the factory masters taught us in their schools
whose letters could not write the holy names
we shout in joy as we remake
divinities they've tried to train us to forget.

Their walls are falling
and the hundred syllables
of tumbling master mason Finn
are waking memories of what we were
before we began to measure out our lives
with coins instead of grain.

It is not easy, this rebirth;
not all the hurt
can blame their clockwork hearts for running down.
So many of us have learned to love this leper earth,
the window-bars that shut our minds from alien kin,
the doctors with their knives and chemicals and shocks,
that life without the walls
might sear our skin
like sun on dungeoned eyes.

When I came down from mountains
to be king
I led you out of the garden
along a new-trod avenue of crucifixes
into the factory furnace mouth
that led to Buchenwald.
As your priest
I comforted you with falsehoods
telling you truths about the gods you once had been
as if I spoke of someone else.
They told you god had died
(it was you they spoke of, and they lied).
My poet's tongue agreed

and I made my goddess strip
and dance for men who made the money mills grind small.
They rewarded me
with salt-sea death in Shelley's mouth,
the dark of Reading gaol,
the gun into my Mayakovsky hands,
for as the last screw turned
into the great machine
they thought
there was no need of magic any more
to keep it running smooth.
My melodies were grit now
reminding you of paradises lost
and promises unkept,
giving a rhythm to your fists
beating upon the locked exit from the factory,
disturbing the masters' dreams
with nightmares of your escape.

You need not beat so loudly
for the lock is broken by my song already
and all you have to do
is walk outside the millgates
and then
back into the garden.

The long journey is ending
and I am forgetting
why we ever started out
to see what lay at end of roads.
I cannot remember
why we thought that gold was better
than the sun-fed corn
for wealth.
Why did we start to write the magic out of words?
Why did I stop singing
   to my mother sister daughter wife's ploughed fields
   and set her crown of corn upon my head alone?

She gave us earth and sky,
her sea and fields and forests.
Why did we feel a fence would give us ownership
of such a little part
by keeping others out?

It does not matter.
What is important is the song
I've sung us here so far,
and must not lose my voice this late.
All need songs
to soothe blood-blistered feet and broken hearts
but there is no way
for me to reach at once
to all of my footsore community
but only one by one
the hymn of joy you taught me,
hoping they can learn as well
the worship of themselves as gods and goddesses.

. . .

We grow like cells:
each within each
develops in the same slow way.
I stand alone
but could not be myself
if your hand had not led me to your life.
Our children rise around us
and as we die burst out into their own young blossom.
The fields our families grow in have been fenced
but soon their flowers spread across the fallen walls
between them and their brother lands.

The same slow way
ruled by the smallest part
so each can harvest its fullest grain,
thrusting its goodness out in wider, wider circles.

The hardest part is learning how to grow.

ACKNOWLEDGEMENTS

THE CLOSEST thing we've got yet to McLuhan's 'global village' is the pop community. The communications are instantaneous, from Margaret Street to St Marks Place to L.A. It's hard sometimes to know how one learns what one knows: reported fact counts for just as much as direct experience. So this book would have been impossible without that worldwide network of friends and acquaintances in music, many of whom will disagree strongly with my conclusions, I'm sure.

I would like to thank Austin John Marshall specially for the chance to hear the tape of the Jimi Hendrix interview made while making the film, 'Experience' and Steve Sparkes for his comments on the manuscript as each chapter was completed.

The book would have been equally impossible were it not for the pop press which have documented pop more efficiently than any other cultural phenomenon in history, notably *Rolling Stone* and *Melody Maker*. I have been associated with the latter paper for over a decade and much of what little I know of pop has been gained in the course of that work. It is interesting that though both are basically 'straight' papers, and the MM is owned by the mighty International Publishing Corporation to boot, they are better reflections of the growing pop culture than any of the so-called 'underground' press. Each supplements the service given by the other as a newspaper of record and criticism. Though direct quotations are attributed to the paper concerned wherever possible, throughout the book are facts that I would not know if I had not read them there. In particular, the *Rolling Stone* account of Altamont in its issue of January 30, 1970, though it comes in for some criticism from me, must stand as a superb job of reporting worthy of the best traditions of straight journalism. Much of the background throughout was culled from the files of the *Melody Maker* and I would like to thank the editor, Ray Coleman, and Roy Birchall for their help in this respect.

Other magazines drawn upon include *Red Mole*, for the John Lennon interview, which was also reprinted in *Cream*; *Playboy*, which printed an interview with Marshall McLuhan in March 1969; the *New Yorker* for Nat Hentoff's profile of Bob Dylan in its issue for October 24, 1964; *Sing Out!*, notably for the Bob Dylan interview in October/November 1968; *East Village Other*, New York, for the writings of Alan J. Weberman, many of which have been reprinted in *International Times*; *Broadside* magazine's interview with Phil Ochs on October 15, 1965, also reprinted in 'The War is Over' by Phil Ochs (Barricade Music, New York, 1965); *Encounter*, August 1969, for the George Steiner essay, and the *Nation*, for Robert Hatch's description of Jagger in 'Gimme Shelter'.

It is an indication of the healthy state of rock and roll so far that is has so few reference books of any worth. Of those that do exist, the only two I have found of any real help in checking facts for this book were Charlie Gillett's encyclopedic 'The Sound of the City: The Rise of Rock and Roll' (Outerbridge & Dienstfrey, New York, 1970), and Graham Wood's 'An A–Z of Rock and Roll' (Studio Vista, 1971). Other books drawn upon, but not necessarily quoted directly in the text, are, in order of mention, 'Sinatra' by Robin Douglas-Home (Michael Joseph, 1962); 'The Poetry of Rock' by Richard Goldstein (Bantam Books, New York, 1969); 'The Human Use of Human Beings' by Norbert Wiener (Sphere Books, 1968); 'The Uses of Literacy' by Richard Hoggart (Pelican edition, 1968); 'Love Me Do: The Beatles' Progress' by Michael Braun (Penguin, 1964) which they are said to prefer to 'The Beatles: The Authorized Biography' by Hunter Davies (William Heinemann, 1968); 'I Claudius' by Robert Graves (Penguin edition, 1970); 'John Lennon in His Own Write' (Jonathan Cape, 1964); 'Ten Essays on the French Revolution' (Lawrence & Wishart, 1945); Lillian Roth's comments on Jimi Hendrix are taken from 'No One Waved Goodbye: A Casualty Report on Rock and Roll' edited by Robert Somma (Outerbridge & Dienstfrey, 1971); 'Don't Look Back' by D. A. Pennebaker (Ballantine, New York, 1968); 'Freedom in the Air: Song Movements of the Sixties' by Josh Dunson (International Publishers, New York, 1965); 'The Divided Self' by R. D. Laing (Penguin edition, 1969); 'Unarmed Victory' by Bertrand Russell (Penguin, 1963); 'The Function of the Orgasm' by Wilhelm Reich (Panther Books, 1968); 'The Golden Bough' by Sir James Frazer (Macmillan St Martin's Library edition, 1957); 'Blues People' by Le Roi Jones (William Morrow & Co., New York, 1968); 'Pagan Celtic Britain' by Anne Ross (Routledge, 1967); 'Witchcraft & Sorcery' edited by Max Marwick (Penguin, 1970); 'The Sex & Savagery of Hells Angels' by Jan Hudson (New English Library, 1967).

Song lyrics quoted in the text, mostly very briefly, are (in order of reference): 'Midnight Rambler' by Mick Jagger & Keith Richard (Essex Music); 'America Drinks and Goes Home' by Frank Zappa (Frank Zappa Music Co., 1967) reprinted with the comment by Zappa from *International Times*, August 31, 1967; 'Shake Rattle & Roll' by Charles Calhoun and Joe Turner (Progressive Music Publishing, 1954); 'Blue Suede Shoes' by Carl Perkins (BMI); 'Can't Help Falling in Love' by George Weiss; 'She Loves You' by Lennon and McCartney (Northern Songs); 'Bama talking to Alan Lomax (Essex Music, 1957); 'Penny Lane' by Lennon & McCartney (Northern Songs, 1967); 'I Am the Walrus' by Lennon & McCartney (Northern Songs, 1967); 'Blue Jay Way' by George Harrison (Northern Songs, 1967); 'With God on Our Side' by Bob Dylan (M. Witmark & Sons, 1963); 'Norwegian Wood' by Lennon & McCartney

(Northern Songs, 1965); 'Play With Fire' by Nanker Phelge (Nanker Phelge, 1965); 'She's Leaving Home' by Lennon & McCartney (Northern Songs, 1967); 'Street Fighting Man' by Mick Jagger & Keith Richard (Gideon Music, 1968); 'Let It Be' by Lennon & McCartney (Northern Songs); 'Instant Karma' by John Lennon (Northern Songs); 'Crazy John' by Tom Paxton (Deep Fork Music, 1970); 'Glass Onion' by Lennon & McCartney (Northern Songs); 'Working Class Hero' by John Lennon (Northern Songs*, 1970); 'I Found Out' by John Lennon (Northern Songs*, 1970); 'God' by John Lennon (Northern Songs*, 1970); 'It's Alright Ma, I'm Only Bleeding' by Bob Dylan (M. Witmark & Sons, 1965); 'Bob Dylan's 115th Dream' by Bob Dylan (M. Witmark & Sons, 1965); 'Positively Fourth Street' by Bob Dylan (Kinney Music Ltd.); 'Five to One' by the Doors (Doors Music Co.); 'Chimes of Freedom' by Bob Dylan (M. Witmark & Sons, 1964); 'Too Much Monkey Business' by Chuck Berry (Jewel, 1960); 'Subterranean Homesick Blues' by Bob Dylan (M. Witmark & Sons, 1965); 'A Day in the Life' by Lennon & McCartney (Northern Songs, 1967); 'For the Benefit of Mr Kite' by Lennon & McCartney (Northern Songs, 1967); 'It Ain't Me, Babe' by Bob Dylan (M. Witmark & Sons, 1964); 'Sympathy for the Devil' by Mick Jagger & Keith Richard (Gideon Music, 1968).

* Also claimed by Maclen (Music).

INDEX